EVANGELISM OLD AND NEW

God's Search for Man in all Ages

By A. C. DIXON

AUTHOR OF
"HEAVEN ON EARTH"
"PRESENT-DAY LIFE AND RELIGION," ETC.

WIPF & STOCK · Eugene, Oregon

Wipf and Stock Publishers
199 W 8th Ave, Suite 3
Eugene, OR 97401

Evangelism Old and New
By Dixon, A. C.
ISBN 13: 978-1-5326-7993-3
Publication date 1/25/2019
Previously published by American Tract Society, 1905

TO MY WIFE
*whose faith in the truths of this book
has been strong, constant, and inspiring*

PREFACE.

There is an evangelistic atmosphere in the religious world. The work of the Holy Spirit through evangelists, pastors and churches in Australia and Wales has contradicted the statement that the old time revival is a thing of the past. In cities of Great Britain and America evangelistic campaigns have resulted in the conversion of thousands. Indeed, such movements have become so common that they are scarcely noticed by the secular press outside the cities in which they exist.

The reaction against the destructive "Higher Criticism" is not only re-establishing faith in the Word of God, but it is also rekindling the fires of religious enthusiasm which have been smouldering for years under the ashes of academic unbelief. Agnosticism is dead and buried. The more subtle heresies of Unitarianism, Christian Science, Theosophy and Spiritualism, denying the fall of man, the need of redemption, the deity of Christ, and even the personality of God, with the extravagant assumptions of Dowieism, Sandfordism, and other isms too numerous to mention, are leading the minds of people to the Bible as the only corrective for all these disorders.

PREFACE

The mission of the evangelist as the pastor's co-worker is being recognized, while pastors are seeking to obey to command of the Spirit to a pastor, "Do the work of an evangelist." The importance of personal work in soul-winning has a large place in sermons, programs of conventions and the religious press.

In spite of much worldliness, many apostacies, and the spirit of grasping greed which to a large extent prevails in the commercial world, the day-dawn of a world-wide revival begins to appear. Let us continue to pray, while we work and wait for its coming.

CONTENTS.

INTRODUCTION.

PAGE.

Man's Search for God—The Failure of Philosophy and Science—God's Method of Revelation in Christ—How to See God—The Process by Which We Become Sons of God—Father, Son and Spirit in Search of Man as Revealed in the "Pearl of Parables"—One Parable in Three Parts—Son of God, the Good Shepherd, Leaving Heaven and Seeking the Lost—The Idea of Distance—Personality—Ownership without Possession—Sacrifice—The Best Way to Care for the Ninety and Nine is to Seek the One that is Lost—The Holy Spirit under the Symbol of a Woman—The Idea of Nearness—The Lost in Our Homes and Churches—Association—Inconvenience—Candle and Broom—Truth on Fire—Dust and Trash to Be Swept out of Some Lives before Light Can Reach the Lost—Discovery and Recovery—Joy...................... 1

CHAPTER I.

THE VISION OF GOD AND MAN.

The Vision of God Needed as Preparation for Entering the Valley of Bones—Wings Symbol of the Divine, Hands of the Human—Union of Human and Divine—Human Controlled by Divine—Courage with Wings—Patience with Wings—Aspiration with Wings—Fellowship with Wings—Directness with Wings—Progress with Wings—The True Optimist Sees the Enthroned Christ 16

CONTENTS.

CHAPTER II.

EVANGELISM TRUE AND FALSE.

The Divine Art of Making People Christian—Repentance and Faith—Back of All Is Prayer, as in Revivals of Peter, Luther, Wesley, Finney and Moody—The Preaching of Jesus Christ in His Incarnation, Crucifixion, Resurrection and Exaltation the Prominent Features of All True Revivals—The So-called New Evangelism — The Times-Spirit Evangelism — Its Weakness—Socialistic Evangelism—Impossibility of Saving in Bulk—Materialistic Evangelism—Prevalent Worldliness and Other Worldliness—Ethical Evangelism—D. L. Moody's Ethical Method—Nursery Evangelism—Good, but Not Sufficient—Academic Evangelism—Culture without the New Birth—The Pagan Source of Evolution—Similarity between Ancient and Modern Pagans—Efforts of Good Christian Men—The Danger Signal—Evangelism Based upon the Winsome Personality of Christ—The Offense of the Cross Eliminated—Satan a "Mesenger of Light".. 32

CHAPTER III.

THE CALL OF THE FIRST DISCIPLES.

By Public Proclamation—John's Open-Air Sermon—By More Private Proclamation—John to His Two Disciples—By Individual Contact—Andrew and Simon, Philip and Nathanael—By Direct Contact with Christ—The Call to Salvation, Fellowship, Service, Transformation and Vision 58

CONTENTS.

CHAPTER IV.

PENTECOST.

The Invisible Christ Continuing His Work—Difference between the Visible and the Invisible Christ—The Invisible Christ Building His Church—Unifying the People—Unity of Purpose—Unity of Prayer—Unity of Experience—Unity of Action—Confusing and Confounding His Enemies—Inspired Word Explains Inspired Men—The Church May Be Too Easily Explained 75

CHAPTER V.

AFTER PENTECOST.

Holy Spirit in Old Testament and New—The Invisible Christ Continues His Work—Using Inspired Men to Preach the Inspired Word—Revealing Himself—The Model Sermon for All Ages—Insisting upon Repentance and Baptism—Personal Preaching—The Disciples to Continue in Doctrine, Fellowship, Breaking of Bread and Prayers—How the Unusual Helps the Usual 87

CHAPTER VI.

PERSONAL CONVERSATION.

Difference between Sermon and Conversation—Get Inquirer Alone—Lead Him to Speak His Mind—Answer His Need—Avoid Curious Questions—Press upon Him His Personal Need—Faithfully Instruct.... 99

CONTENTS.

CHAPTER VII.
THE ENDUEMENT OF POWER.

The Object of Peter's Call to Cornelius—Proof That Cornelius Was Saved—The Vision of An Angel Suited to Cornelius—The Vision of the Sheet with the Living Creatures Suited to Peter—All Should Go or Send—Saved, but Not Endued—The Test Question of Apostolic Times—Blind Telephones—How a Pauper Became a Millionaire........................106

CHAPTER VIII.
"GO GLUE THYSELF."

The Ethiopian Treasurer Drawn to Jesus—Reading Prophet Isaiah—Command to Philip, "Go Glue Thyself to This Chariot"—Personal Work—The Guidance of the Holy Spirit—Ready for Crowd or the Individual—Put Yourself on Level and Enter into Sympathy—Jesus and the Woman at the Well—Preach Jesus—Difficulties 116

CHAPTER IX.
PAUL'S CONVERSION.

An Age in a Few Minutes—Course of Events in Paul's Life—Period of Persecution—Period of Prostration—Could Not Be Approached on a Level—Captain Sigsbee and the "Blake"—Bunyan and Newton—God's Lightning—How a Puma Was Tamed—Period of Prayer—Silent to Man—God at Work—Period of Preparation—Help of Ananias—Telescope in Switzerland—The Test of Heroism—Garibaldi and His Sol-

CONTENTS.

diers—Weighing the Mayor of Wycomb—General White's Peculiar Fear for His Regiment—Period of Preaching and Proving—His Message and His Proof. 13&

CHAPTER X.
REVELATION AND GROWTH VERSUS EVOLUTION AND MAGIC.

Revolutionary Power of Biblical Truth—How a Bible Cleansed a Bookstore—How a Despised Testament Transformed a Life—Sin Revolutionary and Demands Revolutionary Treatment—The God of Nature Revolutionary—Growth versus Magic—Revolutions in History—Teaching of Jesus Revolutionary—Revolutionary Power of the Resurrection—Pentecost a Revolution—Paul's Conversion—Failures of Culture—Bishop Colenso's Experiment—Hans Egede in Greenland—Kjarnack—Moffat and Africaner—James Calvert in Fiji—John Geddie in Aneityum—Darwin a Witness—Death and Resurrection..............................141

CHAPTER XI.
SOUL-WINNING.

The Alphabet of Christianity—Difference between Evangelical and Evangelistic—The Meaning—The New Birth—Partaker of Divine Nature—The Needle of the Law before the Thread of the Gospel—How a Soul Was Murdered—Reformation and Regeneration—The Means—Word of God the Instrument—Man of God the Agent—Influence and Power—Assurance of Salvation—All Ages May Be Soul-Winners—How a Little Girl Won Her Family—Man in Boat above

CONTENTS.

Milton, Pennsylvania — Methods — Preaching — Why Not Sunday Mornings?—Feeding People Not Sufficient—Fishing for Men—Not Cultivating Fish—Sudden Conversion—How a Young Man Was Won—How God Used Even a Ridiculous Scene—The Motive—Love of Souls—Hope of Reward—Constraining Love of Christ. 153

CHAPTER XII.
IN THE CITY.

The Great Battlefields between Truth and Error, Sin and Righteousness—The Religious People Who Oppose—The Imitators—Bad Literature—Demetrius—The American Temple of Diana—The Secret of City Evangelism—Enduement of Power for Spiritual Christians—In the Synagogue—The School of Tyrannus—The Course of All Revivals from the Few to the Many—Pentecost—The Holy Club—McAll Mission in Paris—Evangelism a Basis of Church Unity—The Way to Solve All Problems.................175

CHAPTER XIII.
IN THE OPEN AIR.

The Bible an Open-Air Book—Garden of Eden—Law on Sinai—Revival under Ezra—Song of Angels—Miracles and Sermons of Christ—Transfiguration—Temptation — Crucifixion — Ascension — Coming in Glory—First Church House in Second Century—Justin Martin—Raymond Lull—Augustine—Ethelbert—Wyckliffe's Poor Priests—Peter of Bruys—Arnold of Brescia—Peter Waldo—Franciscans—Dominicans and

CONTENTS.

Sistercians—Complaint to English Parliament in 1382—John Huss—Luther—"Lime-tree Brethren"—John Livingston—Spurgeon—John Welsh—George Whitfield—John Wesley on His Father's Grave—St. Mary's Church in Whitechapel—Carrubber's Close, Edinburgh—Requirements of an English Presbytery—Bishop Aldhelm—Experience in Liverpool—Objections Considered 183

CHAPTER XIV.

THE PRAYER CIRCLE.

Peter and John Mutually Helpful—Power of Prayer Illustrated in Moses, Daniel, Elijah, Paul and Silas, Jonathan Edwards, Spurgeon, George Muller, Luther—Prayer and Work—Carrying Others—Something Better Than Money—Aquinas and the Pope—Taking the Devil by Surprise—The Need of the Soul First—Preaching a Full Saviour—Magnifying the Resurrection—"The Blessed Hope"..........................191

CHAPTER XV.

THE WIDENING VISION.

Climbing a Mountain—Vision of Pentecost—Vision of Paul—Ben Johnson's Message to King James—Vision of Lull and Xavier—Vision of Luther, Zwingli and Calvin—Vision of John Eliot—Vision of Bartholomew Zielgenbalg—Vision of Huss and Zinzendorf—Vision of Christian Swartz—Vision of William Carey—Vision of Adoniram Judson—The World-Wide Vision........198

INTRODUCTION.

Alexander Pope informs us that man "looks through nature up to nature's God." And yet, when one goes into a pagan temple and sees the monstrous things called idols which people without the Bible have made into gods, one feels like saying "Mr. Pope, you must be mistaken. Have not these people looked through nature to devils? Have they not, at least, imagined gods like unto themselves?"

Philosophy by searching has failed to find out God. The deification of natural forces, known as Pantheism, is the result. Even modern science, with all its boasted progress, has failed by searching to find out God. Herbert Spencer's "Unknowable" is the nearest approach to success, and that is a dismal failure. Zophar, in his remonstrance with Job, reminds him that God is too great to be found by searching. "Canst thou find out the Almighty unto perfection? It is as high as heaven; what canst thou do? Deeper than hell; what canst thou know? The measure thereof is longer than the earth and broader than the sea." The works of God, great as they are, are so much less than God himself that we cannot even make them a standard of measurement. The earth and the sea is too short a yardstick with which to measure the infinite God.

A careful study of nature proves that there is a God, since law proves a law-giver, and design proves a designer. The stars shine the glory of God, the flowers bloom forth His love of the beautiful, and everywhere there are proofs of His goodness; but when we are confronted by the fact of sin and suffering, we see nothing in nature that suggests the forgiveness of sin or intimates the benevolence of pain. If we ever learn these things, God must tell us directly. We had never known it, if God had not said to us: "I will forgive your iniquities," and "All things work together for good to them that love God." Nature suggests His wisdom, power and greatness, intimating His love when we are well and happy, but there is no hint of it when we are sick and miserable. If we are to know, then, that God loves us, He must tell us so.

METHOD OF REVELATION.

The method by which God reveals Himself to us is given in the words of Jesus, "He that hath seen me hath seen the Father." Study natural law and learn of the Sovereign Ruler of the universe; look out into the stellar spaces and learn of the omnipresent and omnipotent God; meditate upon the

INTRODUCTION

designs and adaptations of nature and learn of an all-wise Creator; but if you would learn of fatherhood and all it means of love and sympathy, you must turn your eyes upon Christ. To see Him is to see God. To know Him is to know the Father. To refuse to know Christ is to live and die without a knowledge of the Fatherhood of God. To all who refuse to know Christ, God is only ruler and judge. "To as many as received Him to them gave He power to become the sons of God." Paul echoes this truth in the words, "They which are the children of the flesh, these are not the children of God." All men are God's offspring in the sense meant by the heathen poet from whom Paul quoted on Mars Hill,—that is, they are the result of a creative act. In that sense they sprang from God, and a study of the word translated "offspring" confirms this fact. But in no spiritual sense is any man a child of God until he has come into right relations with God through faith in the Lord Jesus Christ. "Ye must be born from above."

THE PROCESS.

The process by which we become sons of God is revealed in the words, "Behold the Lamb of God." We may see a manifestation of God's power and be no more powerful; we may see signs of His wisdom and become no wiser, because

EVANGELISM OLD AND NEW.

power and wisdom are qualities which He possesses without reference to us. But when I see God expressing His love for me in the sacrifice of Calvary, my heart is stirred with love for Him. "God is love," and I have thus become a partaker of His nature. "We love Him because He first loved us." To behold the Lamb of God is to see the God of love. Power and wisdom are His attributes, but love is His essence. Power and wisdom are only rays from this Son of love. Power was even laid aside, that love might manifest itself. Wisdom was veiled, that love might be seen. In the incarnation Jesus "emptied Himself." Certain it is that He was not emptied of love, for, if He had been, He could not have remained Himself. For Him to live is to love.

When the Greeks came with the wish expressed in the words "We would see Jesus," our Lord replied, "Except a grain of wheat fall into the ground and die, it abideth alone, but if it die it bringeth forth much fruit." He evidently meant by these words, "If you see me as I am and see no more, you will not see Jesus at all. If you would see Jesus, you must behold Him on the cross, dying like a grain of wheat which has been sown in anticipation of harvest. The only way for the wheat to reproduce its kind is to die, and the only way for Me to make people like Myself is to

INTRODUCTION

die for them. They may resist My wisdom and power, but My love will conquer." All of which means that the fullest display of God ever made on this planet is not seen in His works, but in Jesus Christ as He makes atonement for sin on the cross. We may see elsewhere the garments of God, but if we would see God Himself we must go to Calvary.

And this manifestation of the God of love was not sudden. We see an intimation of it in the bloody altar of Abel. We see it more clearly expressed in the Passover Lamb. Every piece of furniture in the tabernacle and temple, from the brazen altar to the ark in the "Holy of Holies," was suggestive of the great fact that God is love in His provision for the cleansing, enlightening and sustenance of His people.

GOD IN SEARCH OF MAN.

The "Pearl of Parables" in the fifteenth chapter of Luke is a picture of the God of love in His search for man. When the publicans and sinners drew near "unto Jesus for to hear Him," the Pharisees and Scribes murmured saying, "This man receiveth sinners and eateth with them." The parable of the lost sheep, the lost coin and the lost son was spoken in answer to this murmur, and Jesus goes beyond their complaint. He assures them that He not only receives sinners who come to Him, but He searches for sinners and would lovingly constrain them to come to Him for salvation. Jesus Christ is God in search of man. "The Son of man is come to seek and save that which was lost."

The parable is one in three parts: "He spake this parable unto them," not these parables. So that it is not quite Scriptural to speak of "the parable of the prodigal son," "the parable of the lost sheep," or "the parable of the lost coin." It takes the three parts to make one parable. And it is evident that we have in the whole parable the Trinity in search for man. The first part gives us Jesus as the good shepherd leaving heaven, coming to earth and seeking the lost until He finds. The second part gives us the Holy Spirit under the symbolism of a woman seeking the coin lost in the house. The third part gives us the Father seeking and receiving the lost son.

In the first part there is the idea of distance. The shepherd goes after "that which is lost." The point of departure is heaven, and it is a long way from the glory in heaven to the hills and ravines into which the loving Shepherd follows the wandering sheep. And when the sheep is found "there is joy in heaven over one sinner that repenteth more than over ninety and nine just persons

INTRODUCTION

which need no repentance." Heaven is the only place where there are ninety and nine who need no repentance.

In the second part of the parable there is the idea of nearness. The coin is lost in the house. In our churches and homes there are lost souls—men, women and children, who are not in right relation with God. The Holy Spirit is searching for them, and, when they are found, there is joy in the presence of the messengers of God over one sinner that repenteth. Nothing is said of heaven or of the ninety-nine that need no repentance, for the place of rejoicing is not heaven, and those who rejoice with the Holy Spirit are the messengers of God, whether human or angelic. The angels who encamp round about them that fear God join with the saints in rejoicing over every sinner that repenteth.

The third part gives us the Father seeking the lost son through the famine which he sent into the "far country" after his wandering boy, and receiving him with great joy when he returns.

PERSONALITY.

Let us study each one of these parts a little more carefully and see if we cannot find some hints, at least, as to the method by which the Father, the Son and the Holy Spirit seek the lost. The

EVANGELISM OLD AND NEW

thought of personality is in each. "What man of you?" Jesus as Son of man seeks lost men. He would bring His personality into touch with the personality of the sinner. "Come unto me," He says. Societies may be important, but Jesus was a man, not a society. Organization is useful, but this world is not going to be brought back to God through organization. The individual must touch the individual. Personality is power. We must not delegate to the church the saving of men, but each one of us should become a saviour in the sense that we take to the individual the message of salvation. In the parable of the supper the general invitation was first given, and then the servants were sent out to bid them that were bidden, to invite the invited, that is, to make special and definite the general invitation. God says, "Whosoever will, let him take the water of life freely." Now it is my mission to focalize this "whosoever" upon the individual by going to him and saying, "That means you."

OWNERSHIP AND POSSESSION.

There is also the thought of ownership without possession. "What man of you having an hundred sheep, if he lose one of them?" The shepherd owns the sheep and the woman owns the coin, but each has become lost by getting out of right rela-

INTRODUCTION

tion with its owner. We may own what we do not possess, as we may possess what we do not own. I owned and possessed a good umbrella a few days ago; I still own it, but some one else possesses it. A neighbor of mine owned and possessed a fine overcoat, and he still owns it, but a thief or the one to whom the thief has sold it possesses it today. So God may not possess us, though He owns us by right of creation, redemption and preservation. Salvation means a restoration of the soul to its rightful owner, and sanctification is the full possession of that soul in all its faculties by Him who has bought it with His precious blood.

SACRIFICE.

There is, again, the thought of sacrifice. "Doth not leave the ninety and nine in the wilderness and go after that which is lost until he find it?" Caring for the ninety and nine is congenial work. The shepherd loves them and they love him. It is a mutual admiration society. It is pleasant to prepare food for them during the week and spread it before them on Sunday. They are so hungry and appreciative that it is a joy to see them eat. And the shepherd may somehow have the impression that the best way to bring back the one that is lost is to feed well the ninety and nine who are safe in the sheepfold. Going out through the rain, the cold, the heat, the rough, and seeking for the lost is no easy task. It means the sacrifice of comfort, if not the braving of danger. Pastoral work is delightful. An appreciative people inspires a pastor to bring them every Sunday the best that is in him, and their loving reception of him unto their homes makes the visitation of his flock more of a pastime than a task. It is so natural for him to settle down into the comfortable persuasion that he meets all his obligations in caring for the flock. If the lost ones in the community will not come to his sheepfold for food and shelter after he has taken such pains to provide the best, he cannot help it. It is certainly their own fault. And yet we can read all between the lines of this parable that the best way to care for the ninety and nine is to forget them in our earnest search for the one that is lost. The return of one lost sheep to the fold will do more for the health of the flock than ever so many courses of well-prepared food. It will make their blood circulate faster and prevent that disease which may be designated as spiritual ennui, caused by over-eating without due stimulation. The conversion of one soul will sometimes do more to revive a church than a dozen sermons intended for their edification. And if the pastor continues to feed the sheep without adding to their number by seeking the lost, the

INTRODUCTION

old sheep will in time die and go to heaven, leaving him pleasant memories and an empty pen.

INCONVENIENCE.

The woman who lost the piece of money shows that she is willing to be put to great inconvenience, that she may find it at once. Her sense of ease would have suggested that she wait until morning. Why should she rise from her comfortable bed to seek for a coin which she knew must be in the house? Why not wait till morning when the sunlight will aid in the search? If such questions arose, they were promptly answered by her sense of the value of the coin she had lost. She prized it, not for its value on the market, but because of its sacred associations. It was, doubtless, given her on her bridal day by one whom she loved all the more now that he was out of sight.

Some things are worth a thousand times more than their market value. The torn and soiled bunting of the old flags in the Boston State House is not worth a dollar on the market, and yet the State of Massachusetts would hardly take a million dollars for those flags. They are not for sale. I once saw a lock of hair in the old family Bible which on the market was not worth a penny, but in the estimation of its owner was beyond price. And so every lost soul is associated with Jesus in

EVANGELISM OLD AND NEW

His humiliation and agony on Calvary. Every soul is in itself worth more than a world, but when I think of what it cost Christ to redeem it, I have such a sense of its value that I cannot wait till morning before seeking its salvation. I must rouse myself from the slumber that would suggest delay, and begin the search at once. If I am not willing to be inconvenienced that I may seek the salvation of the lost, I may take it for granted that I have not the Holy Spirit abiding on me. He prizes the salvation of the weakest far above all rest and convenience, and, if He fills us, He will make us willing to put ourselves to no little inconvenience, that we may help in the work of soul-winning.

The woman also lights a candle, sweeps the house, and seeks diligently until she finds it. The precious coin may be under the dust and trash on the floor, and hence the broom is needed. There may be dust and trash in my home and life which must be swept out before the loved ones and friends whom I influence can be reached. That pack of cards links you in association with a bad institution, for it is the implement of the gambler the world over. That glass of wine on your table reminds your guests of the one hundred thousand men and women who are killed by drink in this country every year, every one of whom began as

INTRODUCTION

a moderate drinker. Your presence at the theatre associates you not only with the rather moral play you have come to see, but also with the great vile institution of which that play is an insignificant part. Your parlor dance suggests a very bad institution which covers the world and is associated with evil in the land, an institution which those who have the best means of knowing declare to be a very Juggernaut, crushing beneath its bloody wheels the virtue of thousands of our young men and women. That cigar may give you some pleasurable sensations, but it suggests the fact that you are defiling with nicotine the temple of the Holy Ghost and are given to the indulgence of a useless and expensive habit which a little self-denial would prevent. Those sharp, hasty words, the outcome of an irritable temper, have indicated that you are not led and kept by the Spirit of Him you profess to love and serve.

All these things and more may be as the dust and trash which are in the way of the Holy Spirit's working, and He would sweep them out of our lives. Shall we allow Him to do so? It may not be an agreeable process. I do not enjoy sweeping day at our house. It fills the air with dust. But the housewife declares that it is better for me to suffer a little than to prevent her doing the necessary work. A decision on your part to get rid of

EVANGELISM OLD AND NEW

the things that may hinder the Spirit's work will doubtless fill the air with the dust of criticism, and may even stir up persecution, but the result in a clean house and a salutary influence on those you would win to Christ will more than repay you for all these annoyances. Let the Spirit have His way. If He shows a willingness to use the broom and sweep these hindrances out of your life, do not hinder but rather help Him in the process.

The lighted candle is suggestive. Truth on fire is what the Holy Spirit needs in His search for lost souls. The cold proclamation of the gospel is not sufficient. The tongue of fire "sat upon each of them." The Holy Spirit with broom in one hand and lighted candle of truth in the other seeks the lost in our homes and churches. Let us co-operate with Him, and the result will be a season of rejoicing.

DISCOVERY AND RECOVERY.

There is not only discovery but recovery. "When he hath found it, he layeth it on his shoulders rejoicing." The woman not only finds the coin, but evidently picks it up and appropriates it. The wearied, wounded sheep lying in limp helplessness on the shoulders of the shepherd, is a picture of salvation. There is no holding out, not even a holding on. The shepherd's strength is un-

INTRODUCTION

derneath, and the shepherd's care is round about it. It is simply a giving up, a complete surrender of weakness to loving strength.

There may be discovery without recovery. God sometimes finds us with His truth or His providence, but we refuse to give up to Him and let Him save us. The sheep discovered by the shepherd runs from him, as is sometimes the case when it has been eating poisonous plants. Helpless weakness must co-operate with loving omnipotence or there can be no recovery unto salvation.

JOY.

Note the joy of the Trinity in the recovery of the lost. The shepherd lays it on his shoulders rejoicing. The woman says, "Rejoice with me." The father says, "Let us eat and be merry." The angels in heaven and the saints on earth share the joy. More important than the creation of a world is the salvation of a lost soul. Worlds can be created by a word, but it takes the incarnation and death of the Son of God to save a soul.

CHAPTER I.

THE VISION OF GOD AND MAN.

In the thirty-seventh chapter of Ezekiel is a vision of Israel as a valley of dry bones, and the vision may be extended to the whole human race. Man is but a bone of his former self. And the question of all questions is, "Can these bones live?" The naturalist, finding a bone, can tell to what species it belongs and can restore the whole form. Man in his wrecked condition is still suggestive of deity, and only God can restore him to the divine image.

In the first chapter of Ezekiel is a vision of God which is a preparation for this vision of man. No one is ready for the work of raising and restoring bones till he has learned that divine forces respond to the call of human need; that heaven has opened earthward, and God Himself is now at work in His world. As we study this vision of God, we learn how God in His search for man works through us for the transforming of a valley of scattered bones into an organized army of living beings.

WING AND HAND.

First of all, there is a union of the human and the divine. These peculiar living creatures have wings with a man's hand under each. The wing

VISION OF GOD AND MAN

all through the Scriptures is a symbol of deity. "The shadow of His wings" is a familiar phrase. The hand is a symbol of the human, and in the vision the hand is moved by the wing. The human should be controlled by the divine. God should rule in the affairs of man. The tendency of the times is to exalt man and forget God. This unfits the church in pulpit or pew for entering the valley of bones with any hope of success. You cannot make bones live by manipulation. Only the touch of God through human agency can do that. In Christianity God has linked Himself with man, and would use him for the regeneration of his fellows. Let God have the preëminence. I like the religion of the old colored woman who went to school at sixty years of age and, going to her teacher, said, "Missis, I wish you would tell me how to spell Jesus first, for then all the rest would come easy." If you know how to spell God, with those three little letters you can spell all that is good.

INTELLIGENCE WITH WINGS.

In the next place, we see in this vision a winged intelligence. There is the face of a man, and the human face is the symbol of intelligence. Reason is here linked with God. Rationalism is reason divorced from God, creeping, crawling, grovelling.

EVANGELISM OLD AND NEW

It is down with the bones in dust and death. It is therefore powerless. You cannot argue a bone into life and action. It was reasonable for Ezekiel to do just what God told him; and obedience to God is always reasonable. There was no conflict with reason when the prophet was told to call upon an unseen power. Prayer is reasonable. It is unreasonable to suppose that a God of love will refuse to hear the cry of His children. And a revelation from God is reasonable. God told Ezekiel exactly what to say, and the breath of life went with the words. "All Scripture," says Paul, "is God-breathed," and when we speak revealed truth the breath of God is in it.

It is unreasonable to exalt reason above revelation. Reason may itself be a slave in shackles. It may be controlled by prejudice, passion and ignorance. The leaders of the French Revolution said, "Down with the Bible, the Church and the Sabbath!" "Up with Reason!" But in selecting the personification of reason they did not go to the University of Paris for a broad-browed philosopher, but rather to a low variety theatre, and, crowning a dissolute actress goddess of Reason, called upon the people to worship at her shrine. It is universally true that men who claim to be controlled by reason apart from God are the slaves of pride, selfishness or lust.

VISION OF GOD AND MAN

At the best they are guided by a fallible faculty, a light within themselves which is dim and controlled by many other things. A ship going out of Boston harbor on a dark night collided with another vessel, and it was found that the drunken pilot was guiding it by a light on its prow rather than by the light of the stars. "A drunken fool!" you say; and a rationalist is the fool who guides the vessel of his soul by the light on its prow and will make shipwreck sooner or later. Reason is a splendid courtier to wait upon the King of kings, but a cold-blooded, prejudiced, ignorant, and sometimes cruel master. A man who is influenced only by cold reasoning and never by gratitude, friendship or love, is as near the Devil incarnate as ever lived. Rationalism really demonizes men after it has clipped the wings of their imagination, faith and hope. But when reason, enlightened by God, is linked with Him in loyal service, the whole man is ennobled and rises daily in the scale of being. The Scripture is then fulfilled: "They that wait upon the Lord shall renew their strength; they shall mount up with wings as eagles." The gravitation of such a soul is always upward.

COURAGE WITH WINGS.

The next thing we see in the vision is a winged courage. There is the face of a lion, and a lion is

EVANGELISM OLD AND NEW

the symbol of courage. Courage with wings means courage supported by the consciousness of God's presence and power; a courage quick to respond to the impulses of the Spirit. Such courage is needed in the presence of danger and difficulty. Men who are brave before danger are sometimes cowards before difficulties. God said to Joshua, as He sent him to battle, "Be of good courage," and to Solomon, as he faced the difficulties of building the temple, "Be of good courage." Solomon needed courage for temple-building as much as Joshua needed it for the battle.

There is no danger in facing a valley of bones, but great difficulty, if we are commissioned with the work of transforming them into men. Destruction is easier than construction. I would rather undertake the task of turning an army into bones than bones into an army. A vandal with a hammer can go into an art gallery and destroy more in an hour than a master artist can replace in a year. But with God, construction, though it be an act of creation, is as easy as destruction. With Him there are no difficulties, and when we are linked with Him by a living union we may be as bold as a lion in facing the humanly impossible. The pioneers of this country were men and women brave before danger and difficulty. The Pilgrims who landed at Plymouth Rock and the Cavaliers

VISION OF GOD AND MAN

who landed at Jamestown needed courage for great danger and greater difficulties. When Chauncey Depew made the witty remark that the Pilgrims landed first upon their knees and then upon the aborigines, he gave the philosophy of their success. They were men who lived much upon their knees, and were thus ready for the dangers from the aborigines and the greater difficulties which came in the form of an inhospitable climate, failure of crops, physical disease, and internal dissensions. The heroes in industry may be braver than the heroes of battle.

PATIENCE WITH WINGS.

As we look again at the vision, we see a winged patience. There is the face of an ox, and the ox is the symbol of patient toil. He bears the yoke, and his mission is the unpoetic one of doing the dusty, humdrum drudgery of life. God links Himself with man, not for the great crises only, but for the work that wears by its friction and tires by its drudgery. Henry Stanley declared that he did not fear elephants in Africa, but "jiggers," the little microscopic insects that got under the nails of his men and killed them. He could meet elephants in the open and protect himself against them, but the contemptible little jigger did its work of poisoning so insidiously that it could hardly be detected. For my part I would rather meet a Bengal tiger, if I had a Remington rifle, than to fight Jersey mosquitoes an hour. Meeting the tiger appeals to the heroic in one, but the attack of the mosquito only irritates and worries. If the truth were written on many a tombstone, the epitaph would read, "Died of jiggers and mosquito bites." More people are killed by bother and worry and the humdrum of drudgery than by great calamities. The comfort I bring you is that God is with us in the ox-like drudgery and irritating commonplaces of life. His presence gives wings to the tired toiler. It is the ox without wings that is apt to suffer from nervous collapse.

One of Murillo's pictures represents a kitchen scene with a woman cooking dinner, and as you look more closely you note that angels are in the kitchen helping her. A still closer inspection reveals the fact that the woman is herself an angel. The artist meant to teach that it is as angelic to cook a good dinner as to shine in the social circle or sit on a throne; that doing well the drudgery of life marks the angelic nature. As you read through the book of Ezekiel, you will find that, when this vision occurs again, the face of the ox has dropped out and in its place is the face of an angel, as if God Himself would teach us that the ox-like na-

VISION OF GOD AND MAN

ture, which does well the drudgery of life, is after all truly angelic.

Our God notes the sparrow's fall, and He is concerned with the minutiae of our little lives. Such a God is needed by the man who has been led by the hand of Providence and set down "in the midst of the valley which is full of bones." The missionary on the foreign field, with pagan death all around him; the Christian worker on the frontier, standing among the bones of character dumped from great cities; the business man on a board of managers, the majority of whom are dead to righteousness; the loyal Christian woman, surrounded by the gilded death of worldly society; the honest politician working with those whose one thought is the spoils of office; the college student in the atmosphere of academic indifference and scepticism; indeed, every man who, having been quickened by the life of God, seeks to express that life in the midst of death, and so express it as to carry life to others, needs the patience of the ox with the wisdom, power and sympathy of God. And our God in Christ furnishes all these every moment to those who trust and abide in Him.

ASPIRATION WITH WINGS.

Another glance at the vision reveals a winged aspiration. There is the face of the eagle, and the eagle is a symbol of aspiration. It is the eagle's nature to soar, and in its loftiest flight it rises above dust and cloud, that it may bask in the clear, pure light of the sun. There is an aspiration, not uncommon in these modern days, which would simply advance on swift wings. Its ambition is to keep up with the times. Like some birds, it flies low and parallel with the earth, till it drops again into the dust. It never soars. The upward flight of the soul towards God in holy contemplation, adoration and praise, may not yield financial returns, but it pays if one wishes to cultivate high thinking and high character. Only the life of God can make a bone, whose nature is to lie in the dust, aspire for anything higher. Through Christ there comes to dead humanity this eagle nature.

FELLOWSHIP WITH WINGS.

Next in the vision we see a winged fellowship. The wings are joined together. In our practical age we should doubtless have joined the hands. We are apt to think that if we can get together for work, it is all that is necessary. Federation and syndication are the order of the day. But there is need of an unseen spiritual union. If we are joined in a living union with God we can easily work together, for then the same spirit of love

VISION OF GOD AND MAN

inspires us all. When the wings move, the hands joined to them cannot remain idle. The bonds which bind together lovers of God are not made of external organizations, important as they are, but of inward spirit. There may be unity of spirit with diversity of gifts, and this unity of spirit is brought about not by external coöperation but by inward experience. It is very needful that all spiritual people should in some way be united in heart and move together, if the valley of bones about us is to be transformed into living beings.

Years ago in the old country meetinghouse, while my father preached the gospel of salvation through Christ, I accepted Him as my Saviour from all sin and the dry bones of my dead spiritual nature were quickened into life. Since then I have been separated many miles from the plain country people who wept over sin with me that day, and then rejoiced with me in salvation, but I find, when I meet them now, that we still have this hope and joy in common. Many of them have remained on their farms, and I have drifted over the world, but we have not gone apart in the faith that meets the deep needs of the soul, so deep that the learning of a little Greek, Latin, science and history does not affect them at all. And when a short time ago the friends of my childhood wept with me again as they strewed flowers upon the grave of my mother,

EVANGELISM OLD AND NEW

I felt as never before that we had experiences in common which neither life nor death will ever change.

DIRECTNESS WITH WINGS.

We see here, also, a winged directness. The living creatures of the vision moved in straight lines. In nature the curve is the line of grace and beauty, but in the realm of morals it is always the straight line. God would have us upright, outright and downright. Diplomacy, which is the art of doing things by indirection, is not among the Christian graces. Bismarck advised a company of young diplomats always to tell the truth because nobody would believe them. A Russian officer said, "I would die for my Czar, and of course I would lie for him."

This diplomatic spirit prevails to a large extent in politics and commerce, and we have seen tendencies towards it in religious circles. There is a temptation to whitewash or galvanize the bones by a process of culture, rather than speak God's word and expect Him through it to give them life. Education is considered by some a prerequisite to regeneration, while, according to God's plan, regeneration is the basis of all true education. The first thing every person on this earth, ignorant or cultured, needs to do is to take into his heart the

VISION OF GOD AND MAN

life of God which builds character. Truthfulness, chastity, sobriety, honesty in paying debts, and loyalty to principle in politics and business are the straight lines along which the life of God propels His people.

STABILITY WITH WINGS.

There is also a winged stability. These peculiar creatures have feet like a calf's foot. The Psalmist says, "He maketh my feet like hind's feet." The feet of the hind and the calf are alike, and both are made for climbing slippery and dangerous places. The hind's foot gives stability in action. It enables the hind to be stable while moving. It can poise itself on the edge of the precipice or leap from boulder to boulder without falling. Man's foot looks as if it were made for backsliding. He needs to be guided and supported every moment by divine grace. The Psalmist says again, "He set my feet upon a rock and established my goings." Standing and going are here equally established. Activity does not imply instability. Work for God and humanity does not take the place of conviction for truth. The Christian stands for something while he does something.

There has grown up in some quarters the spirit of a creedless creed. The conviction of some is that you need have no conviction. Their belief is that one need not believe. "No matter what you believe," they say, "provided you do good." As well say, "No matter what you eat, provided you take exercise," for man's creed makes the man. "As a man thinketh, so is he." If he believes nothing, he will become nothing. Some time ago I was invited by an infidel society of New York to address them on "Christ and Him Crucified." In the discussion that followed, one of the speakers, a Christian Scientist, said, "We worship the everlasting IT." I could but reply that there is a universal law that people become like the object of their worship, and if they keep on worshiping "the everlasting IT" they will sooner or later become a lot of "Its."

PROGRESS WITH WINGS.

Finally, we have a vision of winged progress. The prophet sees wheels within wheels. The wheel is the symbol of progress. Civilization goes forward on wheels. These wheels rested upon the earth, evidently symbolizing the organizations of earth which are needful to carry out the purposes of heaven. They are large and complicated. Some of the wheels are so large that they are dreadful and full of eyes. All the wisdom and power of man are in them; and God will have us make large plans for His glory. Not a few Christians form

VISION OF GOD AND MAN

vast commercial schemes, so large that they are dreadful, for their own enrichment, but when they are placed on committees for aggressive Christian work they meet and spend their time playing with pinwheels. They think for themselves in thousands and millions, while they think for God only in dimes and dollars. In some towns and cities everything has been greatly enlarged except the work of the churches. That is still on the village scale. These wheels of complicated organization, you will notice, are under the direction of the Spirit. When the Spirit moves, they move. When the Spirit rises, they rise. When the Spirit goes forward, they go forward. Everything on earth should be under the control of the Spirit of God.

THE BASIS OF OPTIMISM.

As Ezekiel gazed at this marvelous vision, he saw the enthroned Christ with a rainbow about the throne. The rainbow is the symbol of hope, and the man who sees Christ enthroned above all earthly activities and convulsions is the true optimist. He has the right to hope, for at some time, sooner or later, this enthroned King will come into view with power and great glory, when every sceptre will become His sceptre, every throne His throne, and every crown His crown. The festivities of Queen Victoria's coronation week closed with a rendition of Handel's "Messiah," with the best musicians and the finest instruments that Great Britain could furnish. Royalty and nobility were present. As the music began, a lady in waiting went to the Queen in the royal box and told her that when the "Hallelujah Chorus," beginning with the words, "The Lord God omnipotent reigneth," should be reached, all the audience would stand and remain with bowed heads till it was finished; only the Queen according to royal etiquette should remain seated. At the proper time the great audience rose and stood in reverent silence with bowed heads. It was noticed that the young Queen was deeply moved. Tears were in her eyes, her form trembled with emotion, and when the words rang out, "Crown Him King of kings and Lord of lords," she refused to sit longer, and, in spite of royal etiquette, rose and stood with her crowned head bowed before Christ.

> "All hail the power of Jesus name,
>   Let angels prostrate fall;
> Bring forth the royal diadem
>   And crown Him Lord of all.
>
> "Let every kindred, every tribe,
>   On this terrestrial ball
> To Him all majesty ascribe,
>   And crown Him Lord of all."

VISION OF GOD AND MAN

With this vision of the enthroned Christ before us and the experience of it in our hearts, we are ready for the valley of bones.

CHAPTER II.

EVANGELISM—TRUE AND FALSE.

A narrow and shallow definition of evangelism is that it means simply a proclamation of the gospel. A deeper definition is that it is the divine art of making people truly Christian. The divine side of it is the new birth. The human side is repentance and faith. Repentance is taking God's side against sin. Saul sinned, and, when rebuked by the prophet, he refused to repent and took the side of his sin against God, fighting God on the side of sin until he died a suicide on the field of battle. And all who fight God on the side of sin will sooner or later meet the doom of the suicide. David, on the other hand, sinned even more grievously than Saul, and yet David, when rebuked by the prophet, not only confessed his sin, but, taking God's side against sin, fought sin on the side of God, until in his old age he was the purest of men.

REPENTANCE AND FAITH.

In repentance there is emphasis of the sin against which and from which we turn, while in faith there is emphasis of the Saviour to whom we turn. In repentance we think of the bite of the serpent which poisons and kills, while in faith we

EVANGELISM TRUE AND FALSE

think of the serpent of brass to which we look for healing. We cannot, however, divorce the two. One cannot truly repent without saving faith, and one cannot have saving faith without repentance. In a Bible conference the speakers discussed at length the question, "Which comes first, repentance or faith?" As well discuss the question, "If a man named John Jones comes through the door, which comes first, John or Jones?" Repentance and faith are like the Siamese twins, so joined together by a living ligament that they cannot be separated without destroying both. They are the two hands of the soul. With one hand we receive Jesus Christ, while at the same time with the other we give up sin. There is no receiving Christ without giving up sin, and there is no ability to give up sin without receiving Christ.

True evangelism is the divine art of saving people from their sins by inducing them to accept Jesus Christ as Saviour and Lord. We may be unduly comforted by the thought that it is ours to proclaim the glad tidings and leave the results with God. That is true, if we have proclaimed the glad tidings in God's way, with God's power to God's glory. But if we have delivered our own message in our own way, trusting our own strength and seeking our own glory, we are to blame for the lack of results. We are "laborers together with

EVANGELISM OLD AND NEW

God," and God never fails to do His part. However, we may always be comforted by the fact that apparent failure is sometimes the greatest success.

THE SECRET OF POWER.

The old evangelism, which brought results in the salvation of thousands, as revealed to us in the New Testament, was God's search for man through prayer, preaching and testimony. The day of Pentecost was preceded by ten days of prayer. Back of the Reformation of the sixteenth century were the calloused knees of Philip Melancthon and the "Bene orasse est bene studisse" of Martin Luther. "Take courage, Brother Martin," said Melancthon one day. "I heard the children praying for us this morning." It was not the thunderbolt of Luther's anathema, but the power of persistent prayer that broke the arm of the papacy. Back of the great revival under the Wesleys and Whitefield was prayer. The habit of John Wesley was to rise for prayer and meditation every morning at four o'clock, and it is known that he carried around with him a godly old man to pray while he preached. Back of the revival under Finney were the prayers of Abel Clary and the invalid saints whose diaries were found by Mr. Finney to record the fact that they were praying for him on the very days on which the blessing came. Back

EVANGELISM TRUE AND FALSE

of the revival of 1857 were the Fulton Street Noon Meetings, where business men met daily to cry unto God for grace to bear the burdens of those days which tried their souls. Back of the great Moody revival was the man who came from his knees to the platform, and could by his teaching and his example inspire others to pray. The emphasis which Mr. Moody at the Northfield meetings placed upon prayer was the index to his success as a soul-winner.

There never was a genuine revival of Christianity which did not have its roots in prayer. I would draw a distinction between Christianity and religion. The religious instinct, which is natural to all men and is sometimes wedded to lust and worldliness, may be revived even without the new birth. The enjoyment of beautiful church architecture, with a willingness to pay for it, the pleasure of listening to sweet music and eloquent preaching, and a willingness to worship the God of nature, are not proofs that one has been born again. All this may come with the first birth and may abound with the self-centered vainglory of the Pharisee in the temple. But the contrition of the publican which makes him cry "God be propitious to me, the sinner," and sends him down to his house justified, comes only when the people of God are in prayer and supplication.

EVANGELISM OLD AND NEW

THE RIGHT KIND OF PREACHING.

The kind of preaching which goes with true evangelism is seen in the sermon of Peter on the day of Pentecost. The words of Joel are quoted with authority. And the men who have been blessed of God in winning souls to Christ have been, without exception, believers in the inspiration and infallible authority of the Word of God. It is the sword of the Spirit, who does not use men who cast doubt upon its genuineness. The man who spends his time cutting the Bible to pieces has no sword with which to pierce the conscience and no light that illumines the soul.

SOME MISTAKES.

It is not true that the doctrine of justification by faith was the most prominent feature of the revival known as the "Reformation." The vicarious suffering of Christ, attested by His resurrection, which meant that sinners could be saved completely without priestly absolution, penance or purgatory, was the most prominent feature of the Reformation. Faith was emphasized as the channel through which the sinner receives the redemption that is in Christ Jesus, as the pipe through which the water from the reservoir flows to us, but the reformers did not make the mistake of prizing the pipe above the water of the reservoir. Faith is

EVANGELISM TRUE AND FALSE

the hand of the soul which receives from God the unspeakable gift, but the leaders of the Reformation did not forget the gift and the Giver in their praise of the hand that received it.

It is not true that the most prominent feature of the Puritan revival was the sovereignty of God. The Puritans did proclaim and magnify the sovereignty of God more than did their contemporaries, but the doctrine which they exalted above all others was salvation by grace through the atoning sacrifice of Jesus Christ. They emphasized the sovereignty of God in order to show that God has the right to save whom He will, and that salvation is therefore entirely of grace, which is equal to saying that for the most part they preached, like Peter, the death, resurrection, and exaltation of Christ.

Nor is it true that the doctrine of the new birth was the most prominent feature of the great Methodist revival. Whitefield preached more than three hundred times on that subject, and yet even in his sermons on the new birth his mountain peaks of thought had reference to the incarnation, death, resurrection and exaltation of Jesus Christ.

To say that the most prominent feature of Mr. Moody's preaching was "the love of God, because the humanitarian spirit had swept over the land,"

EVANGELISM OLD AND NEW

is very wide of the mark. The love of God which D. L. Moody preached was born of Calvary. The burden of his message was Christ and Him crucified, in contrast with man and him glorified. I heard him say that when he began a series of meetings in a certain English town, a pastor came to his room and urged him not to preach on the blood, for the people of that place did not believe any longer in the religion of the shambles. Mr. Moody thanked him for the information and declared to him that he would preach at least a week on atonement by the blood, for it was evident that the people needed just that thing. And he did, with the result that the community was shaken by the power of God and hundreds were converted. Not the love of God in general, but the love of God as manifested in the incarnation, death, resurrection and exaltation of Jesus Christ was the key-note of the Moody revival.

And these great facts have been the key-note of every true revival from the day of Pentecost to the present day. Paul resolved not to know at Corinth anything save Jesus Christ and Him crucified. And for this reason he could say without narrowness, "God forbid that I should glory save in the cross of our Lord Jesus Christ." It was the echo of the words of Jesus Himself, "I, if I be lifted up, will draw all men unto Me."

EVANGELISM TRUE AND FALSE

A NEW EVANGELISM.

There has grown up a new evangelism which is a strange mixture of truth and error. "Is it not possible," asks one of its leading advocates, "that under the influence of the evangelical movement we may have formed a conventional idea of the necessary character of a revival and the way in which it should come to pass; that the doctrine to be preached should be that of the atonement, that the effect should be individual conversion?" It is plain that this "conventional idea of the necessary character of a revival" has come from reading the New Testament and the study of all great revivals. Without the preaching of the doctrine of the atonement and individual conversion, there never was and never can be a revival worthy of the name.

THE TIMES-SPIRIT REVIVAL.

This new evangelism has many phases and pursues various methods. (1) There is the Times-Spirit Revival. Its advocate says, "It is given to me to read the signs of the times and to understand the spirit of our age. I suggest one may gather what the message of the next revival will be from the spirit of the age, which we ought to believe is more or less the Spirit of God." This is a remarkable statement, coming as it does after

EVANGELISM OLD AND NEW

its author has given us a picture of the times in which we live. "No serious person, whether he be religious or non-religious," he says, "can look out upon society in our day without being depressed and alarmed. There is a general unsettlement, both of belief and of institutions, a weariness of the present and an uncertainty of the future, a lowering of ideals and a slackening of energy—an exhausted atmosphere in which it is difficult to breathe and which is apt to be charged with noxious germs. * * * The attendance on public worship is steadily decreasing, the grasp of spiritual realities is consciously relaxing, the enthusiasm for Christ's cross is fading, and the light of hope and triumph is dying from the brow of faith." And yet, forsooth, we are told that we ought to believe that this spirit of the times is more or less the Spirit of God. No, no. This author is thinking of his favorite theme, the saving of society in bulk; the doing of it by means of humanitarian work in the way of giving people better food, clothing and homes. He would not have a "Gospel Lantern Mission," with the Word of God shining through a transparency, go into the slums, but rather a committee from the city council to clean up the slums and make rich landlords give the poor people better environment. He thinks that the next revival will come alone the lines of such reform.

EVANGELISM TRUE AND FALSE

INSTITUTIONALISM.

One can hardly be ignorant of the fact that this next revival is already here and has been here for some time. The church of to-day is active in philanthropic work and has been increasingly so during the past quarter of a century, and as a result we have the horrible state of affairs described above. Is this spiritual decline due to the prevalence of philanthropic work? Yes, and no. Yes, in the sense that many churches have become satisfied with ministering to the bodies of the people, and measure their success by the amount of money expended in buying clothes and food, sending children to the country for fresh air, ministering to the sick and paying rent. No, in the sense that this philanthropic work need not hinder, but should rather help the soul-winning, spiritual work of the church. It hinders when it is made an end and not a means to an end.

We must confess that as a means to an end it is often a dismal failure. Institutional churches lose about as many as they gain ·by their philanthropic work. The pastor of an institutional church in New York declared that after twelve years of philanthropic work, which involved the expenditure of thousands of dollars, he could not recall a single person who·had been made a Christian and become a permanent, useful member of the church through receiving material assistance. Others who have engaged in such work can make a little better report, but those who do philanthropic work with a view to winning people to Christ are not so enthusiastic over the results as are the literati who sit in their studies writing books and lectures. The worker notices that the people he helps often disappear just as soon as they secure lucrative employment. They seem anxious to get away from the scenes and associations of their poverty. The sight of their benefactors is painfully suggestive of obligation.

WHAT IS GOOD ENVIRONMENT?

A practical worker in the philanthropic field finds it difficult to decide as to what kind of environment is best suited to making people good Christians. As he climbs the rickety stairs of an old tenement, he sometimes hears a strange mingling of praise and profanity. In one room is a family with the mother singing at her work, "Jesus, Lover of My Soul," or "Rock of Ages, cleft for Me," and in another room next door is a family with father and mother both drunk and boisterous. The same kind of environment, and yet the characters developed there are as far apart as heaven and hell. When he goes into the homes of wage-earners he finds piety and worship side by

EVANGELISM TRUE AND FALSE

side with debauchery and profanity. He also learns that on the avenue of the wealthy, where the environment is all that money can make it, piety and worship still live side by side with debauchery and profanity. You need not be surprised that a practical Christian worker looks puzzled when you talk to him about a revival to be brought about by change of environment. He knows, perhaps, of the wealthy philanthropist in New York, who had heard reformers talk so much about better environment for the poor that he determined to buy an old rookery, tear it down, and build on the site a model tenement with water and bath-tubs which he could rent to the poor for less than they were paying for their present squalid quarters. He took great pleasure in the enterprise until he learned from his agent that, before the first month of the experiment had expired, some of his tenants were using his bath-tubs for coal bins, and others had disappeared with all the gas fixtures and piping that they could rip from their places and sell in the junk shop. It cost him something to learn that swine cannot be made into sheep by change of environment.

SOCIALISTIC EVANGELISM.

(2) There is a Socialistic Evangelism very popular in certain quarters. Society must be saved.

EVANGELISM OLD AND NEW

Some have become so noble that they refuse to be saved from a sinking ship unless all the crew can be saved simultaneously. And yet we are not told how society can be saved without the salvation of the individual. Shall we refuse to build houses because we cannot lay all the bricks at one time, or shall we continue to make good bricks and carefully lay each one in its proper place? Shall we adopt the principles of this socialistic school and apply them to the education of our children by declaring that each one need not study for himself, for we propose to educate the bulk in some mysterious way? Is there not danger that this socialistic teaching shall push the wheels of progress back to the time before Christ asked the question, "What shall it profit a man, if he shall gain the whole world, and lose his own soul?" the time when society was everything and the individual nothing, when men did not feel personal responsibility or realize personal worth, but were content to remain slaves in the bulk? If one would be truly altruistic, he must place high value upon himself, for if he does not value himself he will not value others. If a man does not consider his own salvation of great importance, he will not regard the salvation of others as of great importance. Indeed, he can do nothing toward saving others until he is himself saved. The captain of a life-

EVANGELISM TRUE AND FALSE

saving corps would hardly commission a drowning man to rescue another drowning man. A man in the fire is in poor condition for pulling others out of the fire.

MATERIALISTIC EVANGELISM.

(3) There is a Materialistic Evangelism which has its advocates, and it is surprising to find who are among them. One declares that "dying men fifty years ago were solely concerned with the question of what would become of themselves on the other side, while dying people of to-day forget themselves in thinking of what is to become of their wives and children." This, of course, means, if it means anything, that dying men of to-day have not so much faith in God and His promises as dying men had fifty years ago. The dying man of fifty years ago could trust God with his family, while he gave his attention to the home to which he was going; and such hope for the future was a greater legacy to the family at his bedside than any care for their welfare he might manifest. Indeed, it would.be a grief to a Christian wife and Christian children to have the husband and father careful in his dying moments for their welfare. If this statement is true, it is only another proof of the other statement that we are in the midst of degenerate times, and that such a

EVANGELISM OLD AND NEW

state of affairs is either a cause or a result of the degeneracy. But I do not believe the statement. The Christians whom I have seen die are, I believe, as full of hope for themselves in the future and of faith in God for their loved ones as were the fathers of fifty years ago.

I am inclined to think that it is correct to say that a sermon on a hell in the future does not attract as much attention as a sermon on the hell in the East End of London. And yet I cannot help thinking that the absence of the sermon on the hell of the future has done much toward making the hell of the East End. If there were more of hell in our pulpits there would be less hell on our streets and behind the doors of our houses. Sin has ceased to be very sinful. Indeed, it has no reality in the thought of some, and, as a result, sin reigns unto death, wielding its sceptre over the lives of willing subjects. The need of the age is a Johathan Edwards who will picture sin as the real, guilty, polluting, damning thing that it is, and the sinner as doomed to everlasting retribution if he will not repent. Such preaching in the past made men of moral and spiritual stamina, in striking contrast with the soft and flabby specimens introduced to us in the description of our degenerate times. Such preaching magnified Jesus Christ as a Saviour from something to something, and transformed pigmies into giants. Some descendants of the giants of those days have degenerated into dwarfs. They are living in the narrow circle of earthly thought and purpose. They are of the earth earthly, even while they are dying, caring less for the unseen and eternal than for the seen and temporal. Their characters, made thus in an earthly mold, of course lack the dimensions of the heavenly. Is there any wonder that great men are scarce? This caring for the present makes butterflies, not men. It breeds worldlings, not prophets. It produces a race of sensualists, not heroes.

ETHICAL EVANGELISM.

(4) There has been urgent demand for an Ethical Evangelism. And yet the preaching of morality does not make men moral. Whenever in the history of the church the pulpit has given itself to moral essays, there has been a sad lack of morals among the people. Pagan religions have good moral precepts, while the pagans are immoral. The first need of every soul is life, and when Christ lives in us there will result moral conduct. Mr. Moody preached for six months every Sunday in Baltimore penitentiary, and not a sermon was on the Ten Commandments. And yet the warden informed him that the moral tone of the institution had so improved that, whereas six

months before he came ninety per cent. of the inmates were guilty of violating some rule, now only ten per cent. were guilty. In other words, when Mr. Moody began to preach, only ten per cent. of the inmates were moral, with the rules of the institution as their standard, but after six months of gospel preaching, ninety per cent. were moral. A revival of gospel preaching in the power of the Holy Spirit will mean an ethical revival. Make people real Christians, and you have made them moral.

NURSERY EVANGELISM.

(5) A Nursery Evangelism has its ardent advocates. And we cannot emphasize too strongly the importance of winning children to Christ and training them in Christian character. But when we would narrow the work of the church to efforts among the children, or even make that the principle thing, we have departed from apostolic precedent, and acknowledged the weakness of the gospel we preach. So far as we know, there was not a child among the three thousand converted on the day of Pentecost. Certainly the apostles were not converted in childhood. Saul of Tarsus was a man in stature and in the maturity of unbelief. Let us seek to save the children. It means the life saved as well as the soul. As has been aptly said: "An

EVANGELISM TRUE AND FALSE

old man saved is the salvation of a unit, but a child saved is the salvation of the multiplication table." And yet after all that has been said, we insist that the gospel is a manly thing suited to the salvation of strong, mature minds, and we make undue concession to the enemy when we even intimate that the church is compelled to turn from men like Saul, Peter, James and John to the nursery for its future members. The gospel is still "the power of God," able to save to the uttermost.

ACADEMIC EVANGELISM.

(6) There has grown up in the atmosphere of our institutions of learning an Academic Evangelism which ignores, if it does not deny, the new birth, while it insists upon intellectual training, moral culture and humanitarian activity as the only things necessary for this world and the next. Christian experience is explained on natural grounds. The supernatural is eliminated. We are under the reign of law. The Bible is one of several sacred books worthy of our study as literature. Jesus Christ is a great moral and spiritual teacher, superior to all others, it may be, but divine only in the sense that all men are divine. There is a divinity of humanity, and Jesus is the divinest because He is the greatest human that has yet appeared. But a greater may appear; indeed, the

theory of evolution which rules this school demands that there shall always be something better ahead.

This sort of academic evangelism is turning many of our colleges and universities into hotbeds of infidelity or refrigerators of indifference. A young man in a New York town, after two years in a college where there is a learned professor who has written theological books, informed his mother that he no longer believed in her Bible or her Christ. Though he went with her to church and sat with her in the family pew, he refused to bow his head in prayer and took no part in the worship. He informed her that three-fourths of the students in the college had been turned from faith to infidelity by the teaching of the learned professor whose personality was so winsome that they could hardly refuse to believe all that he said. In another institution of higher learning a reformed Jew, who flatly denies the deity of Christ and has not hesitated to slander the Virgin Mary, conducts the devotional services in the chapel. The president of a New England college argued before the Boston Baptist Social Union against the necessity and advisability of sending the gospel of Christ to the heathen nations. Let them alone. Their religion is suited to them as ours is to us. This state of affairs comes to a large extent from

EVANGELISM TRUE AND FALSE

the fact that higher education has adopted the pagan carpenter theory of naturalistic evolution instead of the Biblical teaching of creation by the fiat of God. After God has been eliminated from the material world, it is only a short step to eliminate Him from the moral and spiritual world.

THE BIRTH OF EVOLUTION.

As one studies the evolution of evolution, it is easy to trace it to its pagan origin. The Egyptian philosophers taught that the first object was a cosmic egg from which was hatched their god Ptah, who in due time evolved a world. The evolution of to-day, however, has its roots in the Greek philosophy which flourished from 700 to 300 B. C. Thales, of Miletus, who lived in the seventh century before Christ, taught that the primary element was water. Anaximander, who was born 610 B. C., believed that back of all things was "infinity." The infinite by some sort of process becomes the finite; being passes into becoming, until there results a kind of pristine mud from which all else is evolved. Anaximines, his successor, defined this "infinity" as air, called "infinity" not because of any mysterious quality in it, but because it was infinite in quantity. Diogenes, of Appolonia, contended that in this air there was a certain sort of mind-stuff which bordered on intelligence. Empedocles taught that the primary elements were fire, air, earth and water, acted upon in their chaotic state by two opposing forces which he figuratively called love and hate. Anaxagoras declared that the cause which set the process in motion and affected the end in view was none other than mind. He was the Paley of Greek philosophy, who saw evidence of design and drew the natural inference that there was a Designer. Heraclitus made fire the basis of all things. The soul of man he thought was the purest form of fire and would survive all changes. To him fire was a sort of creator, making and unmaking things at will. Pythagoras, the great mathematician, who demonstrated the theorem that the angles of a triangle are equal to two right angles, and proved the celebrated forty-seventh proposition of Euclid, made number a sort of god, entering into everything and somehow producing everything.

MODERN PAGANS.

The relation between these ancient Greek philosophers and modern evolutionists can be seen at a glance. The "nebular hypothesis" of La Place and Kant is a child of the fire theory of Heraclitus. The "unknowable" of Herbert Spencer is akin to the "infinity" of Anaximander, and the

EVANGELISM TRUE AND FALSE

pristine mud of the Greek is as scientific as the primordial cell of the Englishman. And it is a fact which almost startles us that some of these modern evolutionists are as pagan in their religion, or lack of religion, as their ancient predecessors. Herbert Spencer lived and died a brainy, thoughtful, cultured pagan, who acknowledged no God as worthy of worship or service. Charles Darwin confessed that he had no use for music, poetry or religion, though he was very fond of worms, spending months in the study of their habits. Hegel and Huxley belong to the same illustrious family of modern pagans who ignore or deny the existence of God.

A FALLEN CHRISTIANITY.

Some devout Christian men, seeing that the trend of the times was toward the acceptance of the pagan theory of evolution, felt that something must be done to save men of learning to Chrisianity, and they determined, if possible, to find a place in the Bible for Darwinian evolution, with the understanding, of course, that God is the Evolver and that evolution is only His method of creation. And they have to an alarming extent succeeded in doing for Christian thought what Constantine did for the Christian church when he united it with the pagan state. And as Constantine almost destroyed the church by this unholy alliance, these men, though prompted we believe, as was Constantine, by worthy motives, have placed in the hands of the enemy weapons which have been used for the destruction of the Bible as a revelation from God.

Evolution, an unproved pagan hypothesis, has been the Trojan horse full of destructive critics. They deny, first of all, the fall of man, for that does not harmonize with the evolutionary theory that everything must move upward. They deny the supernatural, because that contradicts the evolutionary theory that the process of upward development is carried on by inflexible laws and makes no provision for divine interference, only in so far as all natural processes are supernatural. This permits man to deal with God only through His laws and links us again with the pagan pantheistic conception of God. The new birth is thus eliminated or made a mere natural process. The incarnation, the resurrection and all miracles must be denied because they find no place in the pagan theory of evolution. Finally, Christianity is an evolution from the pagan faiths before it and is to be classed with other religions, superior in some respects, but having no special claim to divine origin.

EVANGELISM TRUE AND FALSE

The result is a fallen Christianity, as after Constantine there was a fallen church. The academic spirit which fosters and propagates this fallen Christianity has spread more or less from our colleges and universities to the pulpits and pews of our churches, and hinders, if it does not paralyze, the evangelism which had its birth at Pentecost. The hope of the church is in the fact that scholars are beginning to interpret the facts of nature in the light of the Bible. They are refusing to allow a pagan theory of evolution to displace the Biblical revelation. They believe that growth from the blade to the full corn in the ear, the development of life after its kind, is Christian teaching, and harmonizes with all the facts of modern science, while the evolution of all things from a few primordial elements, assuming that one species can be evolved from another, is thoroughly pagan and harmonizes not with the facts of science but with the fancies of Greek philosophers and their modern followers.

A BLOODLESS EVANGELISM.

(7) There is, finally, an Evangelism which is based upon the Winsome Personality of Christ and insists that we are saved by His life without reference to His death. It covers the bloody sacrifice of Abel with the fruits and flowers of Cain.

EVANGELISM OLD AND NEW

It gets rid of the offense of the cross. It dwells upon His character and teaching. Sir Robert Anderson declares that the mission of Satan in this age is as a messenger of light and he would have his ministers to be ministers of righteousness. (I Cor. 9:14.15). He is willing that all men should receive light, scientific, historic, moral and religious, provided they will be satisfied with such light and reject the light of the world that shines from Calvary. Satan as a messenger of light is at his best in magnifying the winsome, human attributes of Jesus in such a way as to turn attention from Him as the "Lamb of God which taketh away the sin of the world."

THE WORLD'S GREATEST NEED.

The world needs, first of all, a Saviour, and then an example. The mission of the evangelist is to proclaim a Saviour. "There is a sound of a going in the top of the mulberry trees." The wind that "bloweth where it listeth" is moving upon the hearts of thousands. The church within the church is upon its knees crying to God for power. There is a rising tide of faith and fervor in the midst of the lamentable state of affairs already described. Here and there in America communities are being stirred by the power of God after the manner of Pentecost. The deep sense of need

EVANGELISM TRUE AND FALSE

felt by so many is a sign of the day-dawn. The very desolation of Zion in some quarters is causing God's people to turn to Him for help. The notes of despair we hear are tokens of hope. The darkest hour is just before day, because the darkness leads to prayer for light. There are indications not a few that the set time to favor Zion has come. Let us strive to keep step with God in this search for the lost, placing ourselves and all we have at His disposal.

CHAPTER III.

THE CALL OF THE FIRST DISCIPLES.

We have in the first chapter of John's gospel the method by which God calls His disciples and the purpose of the call. The method is four-fold and the purpose is five-fold.

THE METHOD OF THE CALL.

1. By Public Proclamation.—John stood in the open and said, "Behold the Lamb of God, which taketh away the sin of the world." If we would make the multitude hear the gospel, we must, as John did, take the gospel to them. If they have forsaken the church, the church must not forsake them. They can be found in the streets and they will come to the theatre and secular hall more readily than to the church. Let no expense or strength, time or money be spared, that the crowds may be reached with the glad tidings of salvation. But in John's preaching there was more than proclamation, there was testimony. Thirteen words are given to the proclamation and one hundred and sixteen to testimony. And though John was no egotist, he uses the personal pronouns "I," and "me" eleven times. He asserts the superiority of Christ to himself and

CALL OF FIRST DISCIPLES

declares that his purpose in baptizing was to manifest Him to Israel. He tells what he knows about Christ and closes with the superb confession, "I saw and bear record that this is the Son of God." With every proclamation of Jesus there should go our testimony as to what He is to us, and the testimony should be as public as the proclamation. The man without a testimony has no place in the pulpit. He is to be a witness as well as a minister, and in the witness box there must be personal knowledge.

2. By More Private Proclamation.—"Again the next day after John stood, and two of his disciples; and looking upon Jesus as He walked, he saith, "Behold the Lamb of God!" There was no need of his adding, "which taketh away the sin of the world," for these well-instructed disciples of John knew what the mission of the "Lamb of God" was. They understood the symbolism of the paschal lamb and were looking to Him to whom it pointed. These two disciples believed in John, and that made it easy for John to win them to Christ. "The two disciples heard him speak, and they followed Jesus."

All of us have our little coteries of admirers and friends. Have we, like John, won them to Christ? Have we so lived before them that when we speak to them of Jesus they immediately accept and fol-

EVANGELISM OLD AND NEW

low Him? How about our children? Has their confidence in us made it easy for us to win them to Christ? Or have we exhibited to them such inconsistencies of life and indulged with them in such doubtful amusements that they have reason to call in question our sincerity when we assure that the Christian life is the noblest and happiest in the world? How about our Sunday School class? If we have won their respect and love, it will be easy for us to win them to Christ.

A young lady in a Bible school requested the superintendent to give all her class except two to another teacher. He was surprised and asked the reason. Her reply was that all her class except two had been converted, and she desired to retain them and seek a new class, that she might win them to Christ. Within a few months her heart's desire was gratified. How about those with whom you work every day in the shop or the store? If you are a consistent Christian, you have influence with them. Have you used that influence in winning them to Christ? Two young men at work in the same office had great respect for each other, and one of them was converted by means of a letter from a friend. Anxious to win his office friend to Christ, he one day expressed the wish that he were a Christian, when the friend had to confess with shame that he was a Christian, but such a

CALL OF FIRST DISCIPLES

negative one that the man working at his side for a year or more did not find it out. The young man won by the letter was H. C. Trumbull, who became famous as preacher, editor and author. The office mate lost the opportunity of doing a great work for Christ, and filling his life with the joy of feeling that he was a co-worker with God in the wide field of usefulness which Dr. Trumbull occupied. How about the social circle in which you move? Have you won any of them to Christ, or have you drifted into their worldly thoughts and ways until they feel that they have won you, and that you really have nothing better to offer them than they have to offer you?

A successful business man in New York went one evening with his wife to an evangelistic meeting and, as they were going home, she ventured to say, "My dear, I was hoping that you would to-night manifest some interest in your spiritual welfare, for I wish you to know that I pray for you every day, and nothing would give me more pleasure than to have you become a Christian." He replied: "I am glad that you have mentioned the subject, and when we get home we will talk the matter over." After they had taken off their wraps and were comfortably seated in the parlor, he turned to her and said, with gentle earnestness, "Now, my dear, you say you want me to become a

Christian, and I promise that I will try to become one if you will show me in what respect you as a Christian differ from me who have made no profession of religion. You go to the theatre, so do I, and you seem to enjoy it as much as I do. I play cards, and you can beat me. I drink wine moderately, and so do you. I dance sometimes, and so do you. I do not lie nor steal nor kill nor commit adultery. Both positively and negatively we are alike so far as I can see. You say you want me to be converted. Can you tell me from what or to what I am to be converted?" The wife was speechless, but that night, when face to face with God in prayer she said something like this: "Lord, forgive me the great mistake I now see that I have made in dealing with my husband. Thou knowest that I have had the motive of seeking to win him to Thee and the church by going with him and doing as he did even when it was distasteful to me. And now I can see that, though he loves me, he has no confidence in my religion. O Lord, thou knowest I have in Thee and Thy work a joy which he has not, and I pray Thee to help me from this time to be so faithful to Thee and to my deeper spiritual nature that he will be convinced that I have something better than he has."

When our friends in the family or social circle see that we have yielded to their ways, they con-

CALL OF FIRST DISCIPLES

clude, with good reason, that they have captured us, and though they may esteem us for many excellent qualities, they regard our religious profession as a sort of fad or idiosyncrasy, if not a weakness they must tolerate. With such an abiding impression upon their minds any spasmodic efforts we may make for their conversion during a religious revival will not count for much. However convincing the argument that you have the right to assert your Christian privilege and indulge in things that are not morally wrong, because you are not under law but under grace, it remains true that the worldly people who enjoy these things with you are not attracted to the brand of religion which you exhibit; and if they join your church, it is because they regard the church as a worldly institution and they are fit for membership because you are as worldly as they are.

The men who really win others to Christ are the Pauls who assert the high Christian privilege of giving up their privileges that they may not be stumbling blocks in the way of others; who convince others that they have better meat to eat than that offered to idols, that it is no real sacrifice to give up the garlic and onions of Egypt for the manna from heaven. Such Christians are the insulated wires through whom flows the current of divine power.

EVANGELISM OLD AND NEW

3. By Individual Contact.—It is evident that Andrew and John started for their brothers just as soon as they were convinced that they had found the Messiah. John says that Andrew "first findeth his own brother Simon," and the meaning is plain that Andrew found Simon before John found James. It is a sort of race between them as to which should be the first to find his brother and tell him the good news. Andrew was not a great preacher, so far as we know, but on the day of Pentecost, while Peter preached with a tongue of fire and three thousand were converted, he had a right to feel that Peter's great sermon was the echo of the personal word which brought him to Jesus.

As soon as Jesus found Philip he went to the home of his friend, Nathanael, and said: "We have found him, of whom Moses in the law, and the prophets, did write, Jesus of Nazareth, the son of Joseph." Nathanael was a learned Jew, while Philip was an unlettered peasant, and Archibald Brown may be right when he says that Philip misquoted his Scripture, for neither Moses nor the prophets wrote of Jesus as the son of Joseph, or as Jesus of Nazareth. Nathanael, therefore, quietly rebukes Philip for his blunder in misquoting Scripture when he asks, "Can any good thing come out of Nazareth?" Philip acknowledges the

CALL OF FIRST DISCIPLES

mild impeachment, as he says, "Come and see." As if to say, "Nathanael, I am not up in Scripture like you. But come and see Him for yourself. Though I may blunder in my Scripture quotation, I have not blundered in my estimate of Jesus." And thus a man with an experience is ready for soul-winning even though he may be ignorant of many things that it is important to know. If you have a vision of Christ as the Messiah and your Saviour, tell some one else about Him. An illiterate cook in a country village won to Christ some of the best people in it, because she had a story of personal salvation to tell and the people for whom she worked testified that her character confirmed the truth of her story. When Robert McAll began his work in Paris, he knew just two sentences in French: "God loves you" and " I love you." He spoke these short sentences to the people as he met them on the street, and began in this way his most successful life work. We should be accurate in our Scripture quotations, but let not the fear of making mistakes prevent us from telling others of the Saviour we trust and love.

4. By the Direct Contact of Christ.—In the case of Philip there was no intermediate human agency. Jesus found him and said "Follow me." And shall we deny that Jesus at this present day presents Himself directly to the minds and hearts

of men and wins them to Himself? It is doubtless exceptional, but in view of this case I dare not say impossible. It implies previous knowledge, for Philip was evidently looking for the Messiah. He had read the Scriptures, even if his memory was faulty. And where there is a knowledge of the truth God may move through it directly on the human soul. Every flower may suggest the Lily of the Valley, every stone the Rock of Ages, every star the Star of Bethlehem, every breeze the work of the Spirit, every spring of water the fountain open for all uncleanness, every path the way of life, every flock of sheep the Good Shepherd, every sparrow the care of our Father, every sunrise the sun of righteousness, every meal the bread of life, and every garment the robe of His righteousness. Christ has given to almost everything in nature a tongue of suggestiveness with which it speaks in silent eloquence directly to the hearts of men.

During a revival in a New England town people were convicted and converted before they came to church. A wealthy gentleman told me that his ungodly coachman, who had shunned the meetings as he would the smallpox, was seized with sudden conviction of sin while he was feeding his horses and, kneeling in the hay of the stable loft, accepted Christ as his Saviour and Lord. The atmosphere of the town seemed to be charged with

CALL OF FIRST DISCIPLES

the power of God. Such is the case when the Word has been faithfully preached and the people of God are in the spirit of intercessory prayer.

THE PURPOSE OF THE CALL.

1. To Salvation.—John was no mere reformer. He did give advice to publicans and soldiers, but it was incidental. The purpose of his life work is seen in the words, "Behold the Lamb of God, which taketh away the sin of the world." The fact and problem of sin confronted him. He knew that men were guilty and lost. The first thing, therefore, which every one needs is a Saviour from sin. We are not ready to follow Him as leader or walk with him as friend until sin has been dealt with and put away. John would have us begin our Christian life at the cross. To the vision of man's need the highest mountain in all the world is Calvary, the only mountain that rises above Sinai.

2. To Fellowship.—When Jesus asked the two disciples of John, "What seekest thou?" they replied, "Where dwellest thou?" "He saith unto them, come and see. They came and saw where he dwelt and abode with Him that day." The first impulse of the regenerate soul is to be with Jesus. It loves the Book, the church, the home, the company where Jesus is welcomed and honored. It shuns the place where Jesus would not

be at home and happy in His surroundings. It yearns to be with Him all the time. And Jesus responds to this impulse of the renewed heart. He invites us to dwell with Him. What an evening of fellowship and instruction these two disciples must have had! What heart burnings of love they must have felt; what raptures of joy; what inspirations of hope as He revealed to them His inner self and unfolded to them the far-reaching victories they were to gain through Him. Now, what they had for one day we may have every day, for He said, "Lo, I am with you always." He invites us to an intimate and perpetual fellowship. The condition is that we go to Him and do not assert the self-life by asking Him to go with us. Enoch and Noah had a good time walking with God, and much of our unrest comes from the fact that we are trying to induce God to walk with us. He is always going in the right direction and He always dwells in the right place. Let us seek His way and walk in it, the secret place where He dwells, and abide there.

3. To Service.—After that day with Jesus, Andrew and John were eager to tell others about Him. Such is always the effect of fellowship with Jesus. It gives courage and enthusiasm in soul-winning. It sends us to our friends with warm sympathetic hearts. It gives us vigorous faith.

CALL OF FIRST DISCIPLES

There is no tremor of doubt in the words of Andrew to Simon, "We have found the Messiah, which is, being interpreted, the Christ." "And he brought him to Jesus." Such direct personal testimony for Christ cannot fail to bring our friends to Jesus, when, as in this case, it has in it the fresh glow of a present experience. If Andrew had gone to Simon and told him an experience ten years old, it would have had little effect. I can imagine that Andrew had in his face a glow of hope and love and joy, like the shining face of Moses when he came down from a face-to-face talk with God on the mount. When people take knowledge of us that we have been with Jesus, they are ready to hear our message concerning Him. Secret fellowship is the source of power in service.

4. To Transformation.—"When Jesus beheld him, he said, Thou are Simon the son of Jona; thou shalt be called Cephas, which is by interpretation, A stone." As soon as the impulsive and unstable Simon is brought to Jesus, our Lord begins the work of transforming his character. The son of Jona has the nature of a dove, easily frightened, but before Christ gets through with him, he shall be Cephas with a character of granitic stuff, resisting evil and strong enough to be a pillar in the temple of God. There seems to have

been a bit of the dove still left in him when at the trial of Jesus he took fright and denied his Lord, but it was evidently in its dying flutter, for on the day of Pentecost we find him as bold as a lion and as unyielding as the stones of Gibraltar. His first view of Christ begins in him this transformation. Simon was usually talkative, but here for once he has nothing to say. There was something in the presence of Jesus which awed him into silence. The narrative gives us words from John, Andrew, Philip and Nathanael, but not a word from Simon. He is too full of thought and emotion to speak. He simply listens to the sweetest of voices and looks lovingly into the most majestic of faces. The "altogether lovely" One has thrown a charm of fascination over the rough fisherman. There is a spiritual mesmerism to which Simon yields without an effort at resistance. He has found not only the Messiah of Israel but the Master of men. Now that the sun is in the heavens, all the stars, however brilliant, are forgotten.

There has begun in him the process by which heavenly character is made. John says, "It doth not yet appear what we shall be, but we know that when He shall appear we shall be like Him, for we shall see Him as He is." God does not arbitrarily bestow perfect character in heaven; it is made by the process of seeing Jesus as He is. This

CALL OF FIRST DISCIPLES

process is clearly given in II. Cor. 3:18, "We all, with open face beholding as in a mirror the glory of the Lord, are changed into the same image from glory to glory, even as by the Spirit of God." Beholding Jesus as the Lamb of God gives us sight with which we may ever afterward see Him in all the perfection of His character, and "seeing Him as He is" is the means by which the Holy Spirit transforms us into His likeness. The process with Peter was slow, because, like the rest of us, he was often more inclined to look at himself and others than at Jesus, and the transformation was thus hindered. But Jesus is patient, and having begun the good work He will continue it until He shall see in us His own image and be satisfied.

When Andrew brought his rough, swearing brother to Jesus, he was doing good ethical work. A lecture on profanity would have done little good. Doubtless that had been tried more than once. What Simon needed was the Lamb of God who could settle the problem of sin for him by making it possible for him to get rid of its guilt and give him an ideal that would inspire him to nobler living. In Jesus he found both. If we would reform our friends whose bad habits are a grief to us, let us bring them to Jesus. He will begin with them at once, as He did with Peter, the process of transformation, and will sooner or later make them not

EVANGELISM OLD AND NEW

only negatively good, enabling them to give up bad habits, but positively good in the possession of Christian graces. The merely ethical method may cast out the evil spirit and leave the house "empty, swept and garnished," ready for "seven other spirits more wicked than himself," so that the last state is worse than the first. But this Christian process casts out the evil spirit and fills the house with angels of light, more powerful than all the demons of darkness that prowl around seeking entrance.

5. To Vision.—"Jesus saw Nathanael coming unto Him and saith to him, Behold an Israelite indeed, in whom is no guile!" Our Lord spoke these words of Nathanael in such a way that Nathanael heard them. If we have anything good to say of young converts, it will not hurt them to hear it. And if you have anything bad to say, it ought to be said before them and not behind their backs. Nothing ought to be said about anybody that we are not willing to have them hear. Truly happy is the young convert who, like Nathanael, hears words of commendation from the lips of Jesus. He has a foretaste of the joy with which he will hear the words, "Well done, good and faithful servant!"

The answer of Nathanael shows that Jesus had won not only his respect but his love and loyalty:

CALL OF FIRST DISCIPLES

"Rabbi, thou art the Son of God, thou art the king of Israel." As if to say, "Lord, if I am an Israelite, Thou art my king. Here is the sceptre and crown. Sit on the throne of my being and reign supreme." The reference to Israel suggests Jacob and his ladder, and our Lord uses the vision of Jacob as an illustration by which he gives to Nathanael a new vision of Himself as "Son of God" and "Son of man." "Hereafter ye shall see heaven open, and the angels of God ascending and descending upon the Son of man." In other words, "Nathanael, in calling me Son of God you have given the top of Jacob's ladder which reached to the skies; let me give you the bottom of the ladder which rests upon earth—'Son of man.' I am both human and divine. In my deity God is made accessible to you and in my humanity you are accessible to God. As God-man I am the medium of communication between heaven and earth—the Word made flesh. Through me as Son of God and Son of man the messengers of your need, your praises and your prayers ascend to God, and through me as Son of man and Son of God the messengers of God's love and mercy descend upon you. I am the real Jacob's ladder which makes not only an occasional but a constant vision of the open heaven and an unbroken communication between God and man."

EVANGELISM OLD AND NEW

Such a vision is the privilege of every Christian, and the secret of perpetual joy and victory is in translating the vision into daily experience. God is accessible to us at all times. He hears our praises and answers our prayers. He delights to give of "His fulness and grace for grace." Through Jesus Christ heaven opens toward us for giving and receiving. God offers to us His best, and it is fitting that we should give to Him our best.

While Queen Victoria was on her bed of sickness, she said to the chaplain at her side, "I wish that the Lord Jesus Christ would come in glory before I die." He replied: "Why, your Majesty, do you wish that Christ would come before you die?" "Because," she answered, "I can think of nothing that would give me more pleasure than the privilege of giving to Him with my own hand the crown of Great Britain and India." The spirit of Nathanael and of Victoria that would crown Jesus king in every realm of our being is the spirit of every loyal son of God, and Jesus is worthy that every day should be a coronation day. Let us strive to make it such by winning at least one soul to Christ every day.

CHAPTER IV.
PENTECOST.

Luke informs us that in his biography of the visible Christ he wrote of "all that Jesus began both to do and to teach." The purpose of the book entitled "The Acts of the Apostles" is to record what Jesus, now invisible, continued to do and to teach after His ascension. "The Acts of the Apostles" might therefore be defined as "The Acts and Teachings of the Invisible Christ," who said, "Lo, I am with you alway even unto the end of the world."

In the first chapter we learn that the invisible Christ continues to work through the power of the Holy Spirit. The Apostles had been with the Lord for three years, and had learned much of Him, but the knowledge of the visible Christ was not "power from on high." He commands them to tarry at Jerusalem until they shall be baptized with the Holy Spirit. Pentecost is the beginning of the fulfilment of that promise, for we read, "He hath shed forth this which ye now see and hear." (Acts 2:33.)

CHRIST VISIBLE AND INVISIBLE.

The visible Christ was born of a woman. He received from Mary His physical body. He was an individual. He chose to be as a man only at one place at one time. He subjected Himself to the limitations of a human being. The invisible Christ is now seeking another incarnation, but He does not confine Himself to any individual. The whole church is His body, "the fulness of Him that filleth all in all." The visible Christ compared His body to a temple, and declared that, though His enemies might destroy it, He would rebuild it in three days. The body of the invisible Christ is also a temple. Paul wrote to the Corinthians "Ye are the temple of the living God." He did not say, "Ye are the temples," though there is a sense in which Christ dwells in every believer, but His mystical body is made up of all true believers.

"When the fulness of time was come, God sent forth His Son, made of a woman, made under the law." Of the invisible Christ it may be said, when the fulness of time was come, God sent forth His Son, made of the Church, made under the Gospel. The Holy Spirit comes upon the whole Church of God and incarnates the Son of God a second time. The Holy Spirit will thus continue to develop and nourish the body of Christ "until the times of the restitution of all things," and shall present it to the Father "without spot or wrinkle or any such thing."

We will study in this chapter God's Search for

PENTECOST

Man in the doings and teachings of this invisible Christ at Pentecost.

I. He is carrying out the purpose expressed by the Visible Christ to build His Church. He had said, "On this rock I will build my Church, and the gates of hell shall not prevail against it." The building upon this sure foundation is now beginning to rise. The visible Christ is the architect who has given the plan and specifications: the Holy Spirit, the invisible, is the builder. Solomon was the architect of the temple; he received the plans from God, and revealed them to others. Bezaleel was the inspired artist who wrought into brass, silver, gold and stone the ideas he had received from Solomon. In the building of the Church, Christ is Solomon; the Holy Spirit is Bezaleel.

WHY AT PENTECOST.

The building of the New Testament Church was doubtless begun on the day of Pentecost for six reasons:

1. There was a great crowd of people. Pentecost was the Jewish World's Fair. It is said that not less than two millions of strangers were sometimes in and around the sacred city. They came from every tribe and nation. In the church of Christ there are to be no class distinctions. The

visible Christ loved the multitude and gathered from among them His followers. He cared little for the external conditions of life, but saw beneath all the soul with its depth of need and its height of possibility. He prized men, not because they were rich, or poor, or learned, or ignorant, but because they were men. And the Holy Spirit now begins to gather material from all classes.

2. Pentecost was the harvest festival. It was the time of gathering in the ripe grain. It was appropriate that the fields white unto harvest which Jesus had seen should be reaped in on this day of harvesting. The Passover came first, and we see in this fact an illustration of the words of Christ: "Except a grain of wheat fall into the ground and die, it abideth along; but if it die, it bringeth forth much fruit." The Passover celebrated the death of the Paschal lamb, and Jesus "the Lamb of God" dies at that time. Pentecost is the harvest, the result of His death. Without the Passover there can be no Pentecost; the dying grain must precede the reaping. The Holy Spirit cannot work in regenerating men without the blood. The altar always came before the laver. No priest was allowed to wash his hands in the water of the laver until he had passed by the altar of blood. When the leper was cleansed the blood touched the tip of his ear, finger and toe before the oil, the symbol of the

PENTECOST

Spirit, was applied. Calvary comes before Pentecost, and the Christian or the church that has no Lamb of God, no blood of atonement, no Passover, will never have the harvest of Pentecost.

3. At Pentecost every kind of sacrifice was offered. Read the list in Leviticus, and you will find that not one of them was omitted at Pentecost. It was a day of fire. And does this not signify that we should yield to the invisible Christ everything that we have and are? Perpetual Pentecost means the perpetual surrender of all things to God.

4. At Pentecost there was an offering of two loaves of leavened bread. At the Passover the bread was unleavened and symbolized the spotless purity of Jesus, the Paschal Lamb, but at Pentecost the bread was leavened, which symbolized the imperfection that was to be in the church.

5. Pentecost was a memorial of the bondage in Egypt. At the Passover they remembered the blood on the door posts and their deliverance from cruel slavery, but at Pentecost they were commanded to think of their days of bondage. This is in contrast with the liberty which the Holy Spirit gives, for "where the Spirit of the Lord is there is liberty." The blood has freed us from the bondage of sin. But does it not also mean that there is now to be a new and holier bondage? The

Egyptian bonds of slavish fear and of the taskmaster's whip give place to Christian bonds of love and liberty under the eye of our Saviour, so that Paul now delights to sign himself the bond-slave of Jesus Christ. And such slavery of love is the highest and sweetest liberty that man ever enjoyed. The Passover on Calvary has delivered us from the serfdom of sin, in order that Pentecost may give us the bonds of loving ministry.

6. Pentecost was a day of absolute rest. No servile work was done; every secular occupation was laid aside. The busy commercial world hushed its noise, and the silence of rest remained. The Pentecostal fulness of the Spirit gives rest of heart. It is the Sabbath of the soul. There are responsibilities and activities, but in the midst of all and under the burden of all there is rest, because when the spirit of Pentecost fills us we are conscious that we have resources in God. In 1870 a messenger awoke Von Moltke late at night to inform him that France had declared war against Germany. Von Moltke, without dressing, wrote a note ordering the messenger to telegraph all the posts in Germany to make ready the army at once, and he slept soundly through the remainder of the night. He was ready for the emergency; he knew the resources of Germany. The declaration of war did not take him by surprise. And so the Chris-

PENTECOST

tian who knows the resources of the kingdom of God will not be nervous and sleepless when he is filled with the spirit of Pentecost.

UNITY OF PURPOSE.

II. The invisible Christ at Pentecost is unifying His people. In the seventeenth chapter of John we find the visible Christ praying that His people might be one, as He and the Father are one, and now that prayer is beginning to be answered, for "they were all with one accord." There was much diversity, for God does not seek uniformity. There were differences of feature, and voice, and doubtless of creed in many particulars. If you had asked John what he thought was the most important thing in Christian work, he would doubtless have replied "Love." If you had asked Peter, he would have replied "Enthusiasm." If you had asked James, his reply would have been "Work." Each one of these one hundred and twenty disciples may have been looking at many truths from different angles, but they are one in the spirit of obedience. Jesus had told them to wait until endued with power, and they were watching with one mind for the fulfillment of the promise. Time was when two of them were anxious to secure the highest place in the kingdom. Prompted by an ambitious mother, they asked for

EVANGELISM OLD AND NEW

a place at the right hand of the King, but now all selfish ambition, envy and jealousy are gone. Self is out of sight. That upper room is a mount of transfiguration where Jesus only is seen. This unity at Pentecost came before the baptism of the Spirit, and such unity the church must have before there can be a repetition of Pentecost. The church that is divided into factions, each part asserting its own superiority, one refusing to fellowship with the other, need never expect to have power from on high.

UNITY OF PLACE.

There was a unity of place. "They were all with one accord in one place." The Spirit baptized the assembled church. He came as "a rushing mighty wind, and filled all the house where they were sitting." After this baptism of the assembly a shower of fiery tongues fell, and one sat upon each of them. We have here the philosophy of revival. God's people must not forsake the assembling of themselves together. The tongue of fire comes as a result of the baptism of the assembly. We may walk with God alone, day by day doing His will and holding sweet fellowship, but if we want power from on high, we must meet with people of kindred spirit and with them wait upon God for the baptism of the Spirit. The history of every great

PENTECOST

revival, from the day of Pentecost to the present, is a record of the Spirit's anointing assemblies, and thus giving the fiery tongue to the individual. This emphasizes the need of frequent meetings for prayer.

UNITY OF EXPERIENCE.

There was a unity of experience. "They were all filled with the Holy Spirit." The prophecy of Joel, which Peter quoted, includes men and women, young and old, servants and masters. The great difference between Christians is the difference of fire and fulness. Truth on ice has no power. Truth on fire will burn its way into the inmost soul. And where there is fulness there is apt to be fire. Fulness is easily recognized. Emptiness is always hollow. The speech of the empty man is as "sounding brass and tinkling cymbal." It is like the resonance which comes from strokes on a drum. I heard a sermon which had in it truth, sense and sound, but the sound seemed to predominate, because of the fact that there was emptiness behind the utterance of truth and sense. The stream that flows from lake Keuka is larger than all the streams that flow into the lake, and this proves that the lake is fed by unseen springs. It is full and runs over, not because of what you see go into it, but because it is connected with great unseen reservoirs that are never exhausted. Such fulness is the Christian's privilege, for in God there is the fountain of life.

UNITY OF ACTION.

There was unity of action. "They all began to speak with other tongues as the Spirit gave them utterance." The man who is filled and fired is certain to speak, and he will speak in a tongue that the people can understand. I will not stop to discuss what these "other tongues" meant. It is certain, however, that the people who heard them understood what was said, and that is the important point. We need to translate the language of theology into the vernacular of the common people, and it cannot be done without the fulness of the Holy Ghost with the tongue of fire. If we talk religion as other men talk business and politics, our utterances will appear to be mysterious, if not nonsensical. A talking church without the Holy Spirit is to be lamented, for talk without power may do more harm than good. At the proper time the whole company remained silent, while Peter preached, and the man who is Spirit-filled will know how to keep silence as well as how to speak. The silver of speech and the gold of silence belong to the Lord, and we can sometimes

PENTECOST

serve Him better by silence than by speech. We need His fulness to teach us when to speak and when to be silent.

CONFUSING AND CONFOUNDING.

III. While the invisible Christ unites His people and builds up His Church, He confuses and confounds His enemies. The outsiders could not understand. They asked, "What meaneth this?" The pulpit and the church are too easily explained. Unless God does something through us which the world cannot explain, we are certainly not in the apostolic succession of power. If business men can explain on business principles all that the church and pulpit do, you may take it for granted that neither pulpit nor church is filled and fired with the Holy Ghost. The secret of the power of Whitefield, Spurgeon, and Moody is in the fact that no explanation other than that of God working through them can account for the results. If the world is able to explain us, it can explain us away.

The wonders that they could not explain, of course, led some to oppose and persecute. They said, "These men are drunk; it is wild fire. Such enthusiasm is not born of soberness and prudence." To them intoxication is the only explanation. Such mockery is better than indifference.

EVANGELISM OLD AND NEW

It leads the mockers to investigate, and honest investigation of the claims of Christ will lead to acceptance. When Willian Storey and James Russell Lowell were students in college, they were opposed to Daniel Webster because he remained in Tyler's cabinet, and these two young men went to Faneuil Hall one day ostensibly to hear Webster speak, but really to hiss and thus show their disapproval of the man and his methods. When Webster rose, however, and began to speak, the two young men kept quiet. They were pleased with his manner, fascinated by his rhetoric, charmed by his personality, until at last they found themselves applauding with the crowd. Their spirit of opposition led them to hear Webster, and Webster did the rest. If the enthusiasm of the church on fire with the Holy Ghost shall lead men who mock and oppose to simply listen to the Christ we preach, they will become interested, charmed, fascinated and won. Oh for the fire from heaven that will fuse us into one holy purpose, give us the full heart and the fiery tongue, that shall make us inexplicable to all who believe not in God, and arouse the opposition of His enemies! In that way the invisible Christ works at every Pentecost.

CHAPTER V.

AFTER PENTECOST.

In the Old Testament the Spirit came upon eminent men and women for special service; in the New Testament He comes upon all, and we need to accept the fact that He is with us every moment. In the prophecy of Joel, which Peter quoted, we are told that in the last days God will pour out His Spirit upon all flesh. The gift of the Spirit is now as free as air and sunlight. He is confined to no class. In the Old Testament the Spirit came on special occasions, and did through Samson, David, Jephthah and others, wonderful deeds. In the New Testament He abides with His people.

THE TWO MANSIONS.

Jesus said, "If a man love me, he will keep my words, and my Father will love him, and we will come unto him, and make our abode with him." This word "abode" is the same in Greek as the word "mansion" in the verse, "In my Father's house are many mansions; I go to prepare a place for you." Jesus simply says, "I am going to make ready a mansion for you in heaven. Will you not make ready a mansion for me on earth? While I am making a heaven for you in the skies, I ask you to make a heaven for me in your hearts· As you expect to dwell forever with me in glory, let me dwell with you in grace on earth, and as there will be nothing in heaven to offend you, let there be nothing in you to offend me."

THE FULL COMING OF THE SPIRIT.

In the seventh chapter of John Jesus said, "He that believeth on me, as the Scripture saith, Out of him shall flow rivers of living water. But this he spake of the Spirit, which they that believe on Him should receive, for the Spirit was not yet, because Jesus was not yet glorified." In the Old Testament the Holy Spirit was not yet in the sense that He had not come in the fulness of His power. He was on the earth, doing occasional service. At Pentecost He makes a full revelation of Himself, and He comes to abide on earth in that fulness. Before the battle of Manila Dewey was not yet; many of us had not heard of him, and yet Dewey was an officer in the United States navy, known to a few as doing faithful service. But since the battle of Manila Dewey has been revealed. He comes, so to speak, to every one of us. We all know of him and honor him. The Holy Spirit was waiting for Christ to be glorified in His death, resurrection and ascension before He could reveal Himself in His fulness. Have we

AFTER PENTECOST

glorified Christ as the crucified, risen and ascended Saviour? If so, we are in the attitude to receive the fulness of the Spirit.

Bearing in mind the distinction between the Holy Spirit partially revealed in the Old Testament, and the Holy Spirit fully revealed in the New Testament, let us continue our study of God's search for man through the invisible Christ as the Builder of His church.

A TWO-FOLD INSPIRATION.

I. He builds His Church through inspired men and women preaching the inspired word. Peter, before he had received the Holy Spirit, might have quoted the prophecy from Joel, and it would have been like the sunshine passing through the ice, giving light but little heat. There is always the two-fold need of a prophecy and a prophet. The prophecy is the God-breathed word; the prophet is the God-breathed man. "All Scripture is God-breathed and profitable." It does not say that all writers of Scripture are God-breathed, though that is true. The writing is inspired. God lives and works in His inspired truth. The man, however, is needed for the incarnation of the inspired truth. The word prophet in the New Testament means one who speaks for God. In the Old Testament the root of the word carries with it the idea of boiling heat. Put the two together and you have a real prophet—one who speaks God's word at boiling heat. The moon reflects the light of the sun, but it is cold light; you cannot raise a crop by it. If the old burnt-out world should some day take fire and give light of itself, moonlight might be as life-giving as sunlight.

THE SUPREME STANDARD.

This inspired word is the test of all other words; it is the standard by which all other books are to be tried. Other books may be as beautiful as constellations in the literary firmament, but when the sun rises the stars grow dim. I heard a learned brother say that he was all the time waiting for light from any direction on God's word; and that is not an unworthy attitude of mind. It seems to me, however, that the best attitude is that of waiting for God's word to throw light upon every other word. David said "In Thy light shall we see light." When I read a book, or magazine, or a newspaper article, I do not bring the Bible into the light of such literature, but I bring such literature into the light of the Bible. The sun has shone so long in the heavens, bringing the seasons in their turn, and doing its work so well, that it may justly claim the right to be regarded as established. No candle, gas light or electric light,

AFTER PENTECOST

however good in their places, should be allowed to criticize the sun. The fact is, they are all children of the sun. They came out of it and have been conserved in tree, plant, or coal-bed, to be liberated by the process of combustion. So all truth comes from this sun of truth. There is a picture which represents Jesus Christ with a lantern in His hand standing at a closed door and knocking for admission. It is entitled "The Light of the World." The thought of the artist was that the human heart is dark, and Jesus wants to enter with the light, but, as you reflect upon it, it grows ridiculous. Think of Him who is the Light carrying a lantern! Think of the sun in its glory hanging out a lantern to help it give light! Think of trying to examine the sun in the light of a candle! It is sensible, however, to examine the candle in the light of the sun.

This inspired Word is an inspiring Word. When Peter rose to speak at Pentecost, he was full of God because he was full of His Word. The Bible is the fuel with which the Holy Spirit kindles His fires. The result of the preaching of this inspired Word through inspired men is that "Whosoever shall call upon the name of the Lord shall be saved." We must not quote this promise out of its connection. The church is on fire. Men and women are prophesying; there is not a single discordant note of doubt; the powers of earth are being shaken. When men in an atmosphere like this call upon the Lord, the call means something. It is not mechanical, but heart-deep; it comes out of a contrite soul. It is pitiful to see an evangelist begging men to call upon the Lord in the arctic atmosphere of a worldly church. If he succeeds in inducing them to call, such mechanical calling may not mean salvation, but when the church is full of the Holy Spirit, and all God's people are prophets, men will call upon God and be saved. The philosophy of this Jesus stated in the words, "When the Holy Spirit is come, He will convict the world of sin, and of righteousness, and of judgment; of sin, because they believe not on Me," and the context shows that the Holy Spirit comes upon the church for the conviction of the world. The world refuses to call upon God when the church has not been endued with the Spirit of God.

A FIVE-FOLD REVELATION.

II. Christ builds His Church by revealing Himself in a five-fold way:

1. In His humanity. Peter began his sermon with the words, "Jesus of Nazareth, a man." To this they all agreed. Every one of them knew that such a man lived upon the earth. The preacher

AFTER PENTECOST

begins on a plane where all his audience may stand with him, in order that he may lift them higher. Jesus was a man touched with the feeling of our infirmities, and, while we gaze at the glory of His divinity, let us not forget the comfort of His humanity. The fact that He was a man brings Him close to us, and makes us feel the throbbing of human sympathy. He was "a man approved of God." At His baptism and transfiguration the voice from heaven said, "This is my beloved Son in whom I am well pleased."

2. From this agreement with his audience, Peter goes on to assert what they will not agree with; he preaches to them the Christ on the cross. Jesus was "delivered by the determinate counsel and fore-knowledge of God." His death was the goal toward which He moved. He came into this world to die for sinners. He laid down His life for the sheep.

3. In His resurrection. "This Jesus," said Peter, "hath God raised up, whereof we are all witnesses." There is no attempt to explain how He rose from the dead; just the fact is proclaimed. For forty days they had seen Him and studied Him, with the prints of the nails still in His hands. The most sceptical of them had been convinced that the resurrection was a literal fact. They spent their lives bearing witness to this fact, and they

sealed their testimony with their blood. All attempts to explain away by rationalistic methods the resurrection of our Lord prevent a Pentecost.

4. In His exaltation. "Therefore, by the right hand of God exalted." The cross is the glory of humiliation; the resurrection and ascension are the glory of exaltation. The valley comes before the mountain, the cross before the crown. The man Jesus is the pure gold. By His death the gold is melted in the fires of love; through His resurrection the gold is moulded and stamped; through His ascension and the coming of the Spirit it becomes coin current between earth and heaven.

5. In His Lordship. "Therefore," as a sequence from the death, resurrection and ascension of Christ, "let all the house of Israel know assuredly, that God hath made that same Jesus, whom ye have crucified, both Lord and Christ." He claims the right of mastery over our lives. He is the King who through His sufferings fought the battle for us on Calvary, and through His resurrection conquered every foe. We count it a joy to crown Him Lord of all.

This sermon of Peter's is a model for all ages. It presents a full Christ, and the preaching that has not the full Christ in His incarnation, death, resurrection and ascension as its center can never produce a Pentecost.

AFTER PENTECOST

REPENTANCE AND BAPTISM.

III. The invisible Christ is building His Church through repentance and baptism. The people are pierced in their hearts. We shrink from such piercing. It is more pleasant to preach so as to please and receive at the close of the sermon many gratifying compliments. Our temptation is to give the people what they want rather than what they need. Instead of the Word, which is a sword piercing to the dividing asunder of joint and marrow, we present a bouquet of flowers and this may result in a large membership as weak as it is large. Notice how personal was the preaching of Peter. The question of the crowd ceased to be curious and became earnest. "What meaneth this?" they said at first; they simply wanted an explanation. Now they ask, "What shall we do?" The explanation and the sermon that followed it pierced their hearts like arrows, and in an agony of conviction they were calling for light and help. "Repent and be baptised, every one of you, in the name of Jesus Christ for the remission of sins, and ye shall receive the gift of the Holy Ghost." A few hours ago you were depending upon Jewish blood, your almsdeeds, your good character. Change your minds about these things and accept Jesus Christ; turn from sin to the Saviour, and show your faith by confessing Him in baptism.

EVANGELISM OLD AND NEW

Repentance means salvation according to Paul; baptism is salvation according to James. Repentance is the internal work of the Spirit; in baptism you put on outwardly what you have received inwardly. By repentance your sins are remitted before God. Baptism does not save or help to save before God, but it is the outward expression of the inward experience of repentance for the remission of sins. Like the uniform of the soldier, it was the outward mark of the early Christian; it separated him from his heathen companions; it organized him into the visible body of Christ. We may magnify it unduly, but there is great danger also of laying too little stress upon the act which proclaims before the world that we have repented and believed on the Lord Jesus Christ.

THE FOUR-FOLD CONTINUANCE.

IV. The invisible Christ builds His Church by leading His disciples to "continue in the Apostles' doctrine, fellowship, breaking of bread and prayers." A great revival is the best preparation for doing humdrum work. The unusual may thus uplift the commonplace. Here is the kind of apostolic succession that is worth having. (1) A succession in doctrine. Doctrine is soul food. The three thousand converts needed to be fed daily.

AFTER PENTECOST

(2) Fellowship. Before the battle of Trafalgar Nelson uttered two memorable sentences. He said to his soldiers, "England expects every man to do his duty." But what distressed the Admiral most was the fact that two of his officers were unfriendly. He called them before him on the deck of his flagship and said, as he pointed toward the enemies' warships, "There are your enemies. Shake hands and stand together against them." The two officers shook hands, and fought bravely for their country. We are every day in the presence of the enemy, and there is no time or place for quarreling among ourselves.

3. Obedience. The breaking of bread, doubtless, refers to the Lord's Supper which kept before their minds the cross of Calvary. This they were unable to forget. It is the cement that binds together in doctrine and fellowship. We are all blood relations through Jesus Christ.

4. Prayer. There were ten days of prayer before Pentecost, but after the great revival, when the responsibility of training converts and reaching out into the regions beyond rested very heavily on the church, there was still greater need of prayer. The church on its knees will bring Pentecost, and Pentecost will keep the church on its knees. "If ye, being evil, know how to give good gifts unto your children, how much more shall

your heavenly Father give the Holy Spirit to them that ask Him." The workmen whom Jesus employs in erecting His church are those who labor much of their time upon their knees.

CHAPTER VI.

PERSONAL CONVERSATION.

The difference between the sermon and the conversation is that in the sermon the preacher does all the talking, while the people remain silent, but in conversation there is an interchange of thought, the opportunity for repartee and argument on both sides.

In the conversation of Jesus with Nicodemus we learn how God searches for man through personal contact and by fair inference we may deduce the following rules:

1. GET THE INQUIRER ALONE.

It is not well to talk on so sacred a theme as the relation of man to God when you may be heard by uninterested listeners. The consciousness that an inquirer is being listened to and criticized will prevent him from opening his heart to you or Christ. Consult him, if you can, as to time and place. Nicodemus chose the time of his visit. He came at night, doubtless in order that the conversation might be private. To say that he was afraid to come in the day is going beyond the record. He was doubtless a very busy man as a member of the Jewish Sanhedrin, and it was more convenient for him to come at night, as well as more private. It is something when you get a man face to face with Jesus, and when you talk with inquirers you ought to be so full of Christ that they shall be face to face with their Lord.

2. LET THE INQUIRER SPEAK HIS MIND AND GIVE YOU WHAT HE BELIEVES.

Christ did not begin the conversation. Nicodemus confessed what he believed: "We know that thou art a teacher come from God; for no man can do these miracles that thou doest, except God be with him." This creed of Nicodemus acknowledges Christ as a teacher with divine credentials, and that, like Elijah and Elisha of old, he was able to perform miracles. It has in it a patronizing tone. Mr. Ott, in his book, "The Fifth Gospel," expresses the belief that Nicodemus came to Christ as the representative of the Jewish Sanhedrin, who had some time before passed judgment upon Jesus but did not execute the sentence for fear of the people. He thinks that the "we" includes Nicodemus and his counselors. They were willing to admit the claim of Christ as an instructor divinely commissioned, and as a miracle-worker, if He would withdraw His claim that He

PERSONAL CONVERSATION

was divine. Such a creed Jesus will not accept. He pays no attention to the compliment it contains, but proceeds to do what we should do in talking with every inquirer.

3. ANSWER HIS NEED.

"Except a man be born anew, he cannot see the kingdom of God." Jesus does not reply to his creed, but to his need. After all, the need is deeper than the creed. "Your first need, Nicodemus, is not that I should instruct you as a teacher sent from God, or that I should perform a miracle for your benefit, but that you should be born anew. You are a cultured, educated man, but there is a need of the soul deeper than culture can supply. You are religious, a Pharisee, who says his prayers and pays his tithes, but there is a need of soul deeper than religion can supply. You have a high position, Nicodemus, as a member of the great Sanhedrin, but there is a need of soul greater than honor can satisfy." Education, religion, position, important as they may be, do not constitute the new birth.

We need not be careful to answer curious questions. Even the most earnest inquirers are apt to be full of interrogation points, and each point may be a sword to parry off too near approach.

EVANGELISM OLD AND NEW

"How?" is the question most frequently asked. Curiosity in most people is very strong. They desire to know the modus operandi of everything. In this inquisitive age that takes little for granted, they want a full explanation. The fact that a man may be born anew suggests to Nicodemus the possibility of beginning life afresh. Many of us would like to blot out the past and start anew from our mother's arms. If we could forget our mistakes and sins, destroy our very personality, and begin life anew, some of us might be tempted to try it, but Jesus informed the Jewish ruler that it is not re-birth, but new birth; it is not beginning as an infant in the flesh, but in the Spirit. If a man could become an infant again he would still be fleshly. "That which is born of the flesh is flesh," and never can evolve into spirit. "That which is born of the Spirit is spirit," and cannot be degraded into flesh. The new birth makes us partakers of the divine nature. We become two men in one, the flesh warring against the spirit and the spirit against the flesh. It is every child's right to be well born the first time; but however high the lineage and noble the parentage or godly the environment of the first birth, nothing can make it other than a birth of the flesh. Better than to be re-born of our natural parents is to be new-born of God.

PERSONAL CONVERSATION

4. PRESS UPON HIM HIS PERSONAL NEED.

Jesus comes now very close to Nicodemus. He lays down the principle that all men, to see the kingdom of God, must be born anew. He tells him that it is a spiritual and not a natural birth, that he may wonder as much as he pleases at the mystery of God's part, for He is "a God that hideth Himself." All life is mysterious. And now He presses upon Him His personal need: "Marvel not that I said unto thee, Ye must be born again." I can see our Lord looking the Jewish ruler kindly in the face, showing great love and earnestness in every feature, as He says, "Ye must be born again. It is something that concerns not the world in general, but you as an individual. Men are not born wholesale of the Spirit any more than they are of the flesh. It is an individual, personal matter; and I press upon you, Nicodemus, the importance of attending to it at once." In dealing with inquirers it is not enough to lay down general principles and proclaim abstract truths. We should press upon each one his personal need, and urge him to accept Christ at once.

5. FAITHFULLY INSTRUCT.

Jesus proceeds to teach Nicodemus three things:

1. As to the nature of the Messiah. "No man

EVANGELISM OLD AND NEW

hath ascended up to heaven, but he that came down from heaven, even the Son of man which is in heaven." In these words Jesus proclaims His own divinity. It is stronger than a dogmatic assertion. It leaves the inquirer to draw his own inevitable conclusion. In substance Christ says: "I who talk with you, the Son of man, am in heaven while I am here on earth. I am omnipresent; I am God Himself."

In dealing with inquirers there must be no flinching on this point. Jesus Christ is God, and before Him they must bow the knee. He will not compromise upon any flattering confession of His humanity. He is either God to be worshipped, or a man to be rejected. There is no middle ground.

2. Our Lord proceeds to give Nicodemus the plan of salvation: "As Moses lifted up the serpent in the wilderness, even so must the Son of man be lifted up: that whosoever believeth in Him should not perish, but have eternal life." In other words, "Here is your part, Nicodemus. The Israelites, bitten by the fiery serpents, at the command of Moses looked to the uplifted serpent of brass. I, the Son of man, am going to be lifted up on a cross, and you, to be healed of the bite of the serpent of pride and unbelief, must look by faith to me." The plan of salvation is the uplifted Jesus and the looking sinner. You are not called upon

to understand the relation between the look and the life it imparts; it is yours to do what is a very simple thing in itself, and God will do the rest.

LOOK AND LIVE.

3. And now that Jesus has unfolded to him the plan of salvation, He proceeds to give the philosophy of salvation. "For God so loved the world that He gave His only begotten Son; that whosoever believeth in Him should not perish, but have everlasting life." The explanation of this uplifted Christ is the love of God. The explanation of the uplifted serpent in the wilderness was God's love. He loved the people so much that He wished to save them from the terrible effect of the poison. He did not see fit to remove the serpents; they remained, while He gave an antidote for their bite. God's love does not lead Him to banish sin from the world, but through the uplifted Christ to save men from their sins. Love is the philosophy of eternal life. God does not love us because Jesus died for us. Jesus died because God loved us. The foundation of our salvation is the love of God manifest in the death of Christ upon the cross.

Observe these five rules in personal conversation and you will not fail to win some to Christ.

CHAPTER VII.

THE ENDUEMENT OF POWER.

It is evident that Cornelius was a converted man before Peter went to him. He was devout, feared God, gave alms, and prayed to God always. It is easy to read between the lines that Philip, who had preached at Cæsarea, was used of God in the conversion of Cornelius. Philip, however, would not baptize a Gentile and receive him into the Christian church; his mission was to the Jews. I am aware that in rehearsing the matter to the council of Jerusalem, Peter declared that the angel said to Cornelius, "Send men to Joppa and call for Simon, who shall tell thee words whereby thou and thy house shall be saved." But this does not prove that Cornelius was unsaved. We sometimes announce that we will preach on how to be saved, or that in an after-meeting we will tell the people how they may be saved. This does not imply that everyone present will be unsaved. The soldiers and household, servants of Cornelius, were doubtless many of them unsaved, and he was anxious for their salvation. Peter comes with another message to Cornelius, but with a message of saving grace to his household.

In the opening of his address Peter says, "Of a

ENDUEMENT OF POWER

truth I perceive that God is no respecter of persons: but in every nation he that feareth Him, and worketh righteousness is accepted with Him." These words are often quoted to prove that a man may be saved who does not accept the Lord Jesus Christ, that all he needs to do is to fear God and work righteousness in the way of giving alms to the poor, and helping his neighbor. But the words which follow disprove this position. Listen! "The word which God sent unto the children of Israel, preaching peace by Jesus Christ: (He is Lord of all:) that word I say ye know." Cornelius knew "the word which God sent," "preaching peace by Jesus Christ." He had accepted the peace through Christ and the Lordship of Christ, and that is salvation. It is a wresting of Scripture to use Cornelius as an instance of a man who was saved without faith in Christ, when we are distinctly told that he knew the word which brought peace by Jesus Christ. In a sermon a few days before this Peter had said, "There is none other name under heaven given among men, whereby we must be saved." Does he now give the lie to this assertion? Has he changed his gospel in so short a time? Nay, verily. Cornelius must be saved like any other sinner, by accepting peace through Jesus Christ and acknowledging Him Lord of all, and this Peter plainly declares he had done.

EVANGELISM OLD AND NEW

THE TWO VISIONS.

Cornelius prayed always. His breath was prayer. He felt the need of something which he did not have. His friends were unsaved, and he could not refrain from praying for them. His alms he gave to men, but he did not feel that this excused him from giving prayer to God. He was not among those who make philanthropy take the place of worship. With Peter it seems to have been a time of perplexity. He was stopping at the house of Simon the tanner. To come in contact with a man engaged in so unclean a business was ceremonial defilement, and Peter still had scruples as a Jew. He may have been uncertain as to whether he should eat with Simon and his family, so he remains fasting. He goes up on the housetop to get away from people and things that would defile him, and there he spends his time in prayer to God for guidance. God answered the prayer of Cornelius by sending an angel; He answered the prayer of Peter by letting down a sheet filled with animals.

God approaches each of these men in an appropriate manner. It is fitting that an angel, one of heaven's warriors and messengers, should approach a Roman centurion. God thus comes to Cornelius on a level. On the other hand, Peter, as a fisherman, was used to beasts and creeping

ENDUEMENT OF POWER

things and fowls of the air. He understood their habits; he knew what they were fit for. They were better adapted to instruct him than an angel. Thus God approaches us on our level. Jesus adapted His teaching to the people who were about Him. For this reason He spake in parables, using the commonplaces of life.

GO OR SEND.

Peter has his orders to go; Cornelius his orders to send. At first Peter was puzzled to know the full meaning of the vision. "Does God intend to teach me that I should eat with Simon the tanner, and sleep in his house; that, as the Spirit has cleansed him, I must call him clean and treat him as such? Is it a lesson for me that I should now no longer as a Jew draw distinctions between animals clean and unclean, and eat what is set before me; or has God deeper things than these externals which He would teach me?" The order to go to the household of Cornelius gave to Peter the deeper meaning of the vision. He is hereafter to disregard the distinction between Jew and Gentile. Whoever accepts Christ is his brother. His enduement with the spirit of love liberates his soul from the shackles of caste.

And thus it is that we ought to be looking for the deeper meaning of God's dealings with us. In

EVANGELISM OLD AND NEW

His providence has He let down before us a sheet full of the wild beasts of affliction, creeping things of worry, and the fowls of adversity? There is in His dealings something more than the external acts; He wants to teach us sympathy with the poor, the worried and the afflicted. Break the shell that you may get through it to the kernel; press through the outer court of mere circumstances into the holy of holies, where God would teach you deep spiritual truth. Peter goes without a question. Has God called you to go to the neighbor next door, to the tramp on the street, to the partner in business, to the friend in your social circle, to the worst character in town; or has He called you to go across the ocean to the heathen? Be certain that the call is from Him, and then do not tarry. Arise and go where He sends you.

On the other hand, Cornelius was under orders to send. He commissioned his trusty soldiers to carry the message to Joppa. The duties of Cornelius are such that he ought to remain while others go. It may be that God does not want you to go as a missionary to the heathen, or to give up your business and devote your time to missionary work in the city. But if He has not called you to go, you may take it for granted that He has called you to send. There are others, true and tried, who are waiting to go. Can you furnish the

ENDUEMENT OF POWER

money with which to send them? Are you willing to give your child as a messenger of the King to those sitting in darkness? When Leonard Woods, President of Bowdoin College, was invited by Louis Phillipe to attend a reception, he did not answer the invitation but appeared on time at the reception. When the king met him, he said that he had feared he would not have the pleasure of his company, as he had not heard from him in response to his invitation. "We thought," replied Dr. Woods, "that the invitation of a king was to be obeyed, not answered." Christ invites us, first of all, to come to Him, that we may have the bread of life, and then take it to others. His invitation is a command. It should be our joy to obey, and no obstacle should hinder.

SAVED BUT NOT ENDUED.

The message of Cornelius was one of need. He desired instruction for himself, and salvation for his friends. He felt unequal to the task that lay before him. Peter's message was two-fold—one of salvation and power. He begins by assuring Cornelius that he knows already the Lord Jesus Christ, and that he knows how "God anointed Jesus of Nazareth with the Holy Ghost and with power, who went about doing good, and healing all that were oppressed of the devil, for God was

EVANGELISM OLD AND NEW

with Him. And we are witnesses of all things which He did." He preaches unto them the death, resurrection, and second coming of our Lord, closing with the thrilling words: "To Him give all the prophets witness, that through His name whosoever believeth in Him shall receive remission of sins."

You will notice that Peter puts first the anointing of Jesus with the Holy Ghost and power, and this reveals the purpose of his being sent to Cornelius. Cornelius was saved, but not endued with power. He had accepted Jesus, but he had not received the Holy Spirit. There are many Christians to-day who are genuinely saved, but not empowered. They believe in Christ and His atoning blood, but they have not honored the Holy Ghost by receiving Him for service. Paul asked the disciples at Ephesus, "Did ye receive the Holy Ghost when ye believed?" and the question implies that it is possible to believe without receiving the Holy Spirit.

And here lies the secret of our weakness in Christian work. We have received Jesus Christ, and are ourselves saved, but we have not received the Holy Spirit by whom we are endued with power for service in saving others. We came to Christ as we were, and He saved us. Let us now

ENDUEMENT OF POWER

come to the Holy Spirit just as we are, and He will endue us. The Holy Spirit within us is for life; the Holy Spirit upon us is for power. Every regenerate child of God has the life of the Spirit in him, but the child of God must receive the Holy Spirit by an act of faith if he would have power upon him. The mission of Peter was to endue Cornelius and his household with the power of the Spirit. "While Peter yet spake these words, the Holy Spirit fell on them which heard the word, and they of the circumcision which believed were astonished, as many as came with Peter, because that on the Gentiles also was poured out the gift of the Holy Spirit." And in telling his experience before the council, Peter said, "As I began to speak, the Holy Ghost fell on them as on us at the beginning." He does not say that the Holy Spirit fell on him while he spake, but on those who heard him. Peter had already received the Holy Ghost for power, and he was abiding in His strength. The power came upon the audience when the preacher began to speak. We are in the habit of looking for power at the close of the sermon. We are trusting the sermon to give the power. If we trust God, He can give power at the beginning as well as at the close, and when the power falls upon us at the beginning, the sermon cannot be a failure.

EVANGELISM OLD AND NEW

THE TEST QUESTION.

Peter asked the question, "Can any man forbid water that these should not be baptized which have received the Holy Ghost as well as we?" He does not say, "which have received Jesus Christ as well as we." That was taken for granted. The apostolic test for church membership was not, "Have ye received Jesus Christ?" When a man in the face of persecution and death confessed Jesus Christ, there was no need of asking any further questions. In this day of easy-going religion it is necessary for us to learn, first of all, whether an applicant for church membership has really received Christ. The test of apostolic admission was, "Have ye received the Holy Ghost?" If you have not, you may be saved, but you are not in a condition to witness for Jesus. You will have no power in saving others. And we are not saved simply to go to heaven, but that we may carry others to heaven with us, and give them a heaven on the way.

There are some business men who have what are known as blind telephones; they can call up others in the city, but no one is permitted to call them up. They use others without allowing others to use them. Christianity is not such a blind telephone that takes from everybody else while it gives to none. Its very essence is to give unto

ENDUEMENT OF POWER

others what we have received, and the Lord wants us to be very rich in grace and power, that we may enrich others. I read some time ago of a man who died in a London poorhouse. When he was committed as a pauper many years ago, the commissioners were told that he owned a piece of real estate in the country. The land was examined and found to be worthless. Nothing would grow on it, and it had no value even upon which to pay taxes. The pauper, however, willed his barren tract of land to some relatives, and after his death they examined it and found that underneath its barren surface there was a rich copper mine. Those relatives are to-day living in a fine section of London with a large income. The man was rich while he thought he was poor. And so Christians may be paupers in power if they do not receive the Holy Spirit, whose mission is to take the things of Christ and show them to us, thus enriching with the wealth of God and making us channels of wealth to others.

CHAPTER VIII.

"GO GLUE THYSELF."

The treasurer of an Ethopian queen has heard from the Jews living in his country of the great God at Jerusalem, and he has gone there to worship. He may have been present on the day of the crucifixion. I see him moving with the surging crowd out of the gate toward Calvary. He stands by the cross and looks into the face of the Man hanging between the two thieves. He hears Him pray for His enemies and speak words of peace to the malefactor at His side. He simply wonders. He is there on the day of Pentecost, and I see him approaching John and saying, "Can you give me something to read about this wonderful Man whom I saw crucified and who you say has risen from the dead?" John replies, "Get the prophecy of Isaiah and read that." At great expense the parchment is purchased, and the treasurer starts home in his chariot with his retinue about him. As he reads aloud after the Oriental custom, a man approaches and asks him whether he understands what he is reading. "How can I except someone should guide me? Come up and sit with me in the chariot and explain to me the words

"GO GLUE THYSELF"

of the prophet. Is he speaking of himself or of the Man I saw hanging on the cross?" Philip accepts the gracious invitation, unfolds to him the way of life, baptizes him, and sends him on his way rejoicing.

Now from this account we may learn, first, some rules to guide us in personal work, and, second, some of the difficulties in the way.

RULES.

1. YIELD YOURSELF COMPLETELY TO THE GUIDANCE OF THE HOLY SPIRIT AND DO WHAT HE DIRECTS.

Philip has been preaching in the great city of Samaria. Thousands come to hear him, and hundreds have been converted. The Holy Spirit directs him to leave this crowded city and go into an uninhabited place. I can see the puzzled face of Philip as he tries to explain to himself why God wants him where there are no people. He might have said, "The wilderness does not need any preaching. I should remain where there are crowds of people who are willing to hear me." But I do Philip an injustice. No such puzzled expression was on his face. He went without questioning just where the Spirit guided; and if you want to be a soul-winner, you must yield yourself without reserve to the leading of the Holy Spirit.

EVANGELISM OLD AND NEW

2. PUT YOURSELF ON A LEVEL WITH THE ONE YOU APPROACH, AND ENTER INTO SYMPATHY WITH HIM.

The eunuch was reading the Scriptures, and Philip began to talk with him about the subject in hand. He sat down beside him physically and intellectually in the chariot. In this he was following the example of Jesus. To the woman at the well with the water pitcher in hand He talked about the water of life, and urged her to drink, that she might not thirst again. To the woman fresh from the kitchen He spoke of the leaven that leaveneth the whole lump. As He walked by the field where the farmer was scattering the seed, He gave the parable of the sower. We must give people the truth, and a peg to hang it on, a handle by which to take hold of it. Learn their channels of thought, and put the truth into the mind through those channels.

3. PREACH JESUS.

The eunuch was reading the chapter in Isaiah which refers to the Messiah, and when you find a man reading the Bible it is easy to begin at the same Scripture and preach unto him Jesus. Philip did not preach simply about Jesus. We may tell where Jesus was born, what He said and did, and yet not preach Jesus. Many Sunday school teachers tell their scholars all they know about

"GO GLUE THYSELF"

Jesus, but do not urge them to accept Jesus as their Saviour and Lord. What this rich Ethiopian treasurer needed was Jesus, and every sinner on earth, whether he be rich or poor, learned or ignorant, black or white, has the same need. It is safe to preach Jesus to everybody, for Jesus meets the need of every soul.

BE LOVINGLY PERSISTENT.

The Greek of Acts 8:29 says, "Go near and glue thyself to this chariot." Take time for personal conversation. Be patient with questions and objections. Cultivate the spirit of the Good Shepherd who seeks till He finds.

DIFFICULTIES.

It is easier to prepare a sermon and preach it to a crowd than to approach an individual and preach to him Jesus. There are more difficulties in the way of reaching the individual than of proclaiming the gospel to the crowd. It takes more courage and wisdom to do personal work than to make public addresses, and, sad to say, many preachers take more delight in public addresses than in private soul-winning.

Let us look at some of the difficulties in the way of Philip, and they suggest the difficulties that confront us.

EVANGELISM OLD AND NEW

1. THE EUNUCH WAS A STRANGER.

Philip had never seen him before. He belonged to a different nationality. They had little in common but sin and the need of a Saviour. The fact that a man is a stranger to you is not always a disadvantage. If your life is inconsistent, the less he may know about you the more influence you will have with him. This explains why some parents cannot talk to their children. The children know them too well. They were there when the temper was lost and the sharp, bitter words were spoken. They see in the private life the defects of character. This explains also why the husband cannot talk to the wife, and the wife to the husband; they know each other too well. If there is any obstacle in the way of reaching those who know us best, let us at once get rid of it. Go to the person who knows you and make full confession of your sin, ask forgiveness, and determine by God's help hereafter to live as you should. The most impressive thing at the funeral of Mr. Moody was the address of his son, W. R. Moody. He rose in the audience and said, "I would like to speak a word for the family. Our father gave us one of the happiest homes in the world. Sometimes he spoke impulsively, and it may be a little sharply to the children, but when he did so he always called us up afterwards and begged our pardon. That was D.

"GO GLUE THYSELF"

L. Moody in the home." And when we heard this testimony from the lips of his son, the great evangelist seemed to be greater still. It is noble to confess our faults one to another. If you feel that you have not been living as you should before those whom you love, do not let the sun go down before you confess the sin of it and seek their salvation.

It is encouraging to a Christian worker to know that he may be used of God in saving the stranger. Let not the fact that he is a stranger keep you from approaching him and telling him of Jesus. The Spirit may be moving upon his heart as upon the heart of the eunuch in preparing the way.

2. THE EUNUCH WAS PREOCCUPIED.

He was very busy reading the Bible, and we were taught in childhood that it is impolite to interrupt one while he is reading. And yet Philip pressed his way through this barrier of preoccupation, and preached unto him Jesus. This is a busy age. Men and women about us are preoccupied with their temporal affairs. Some of them are oppressed by the burden of wealth; others by poverty. The business man in his office has many callers and cares. Shall we go in and thrust ourselves upon him while he is thus preoccupied? Shall we tell him there is one thing more impor-

EVANGELISM OLD AND NEW

tant than making money? He knows it before you tell him. He will honor you for your earnest persistence.

While I was preaching in a Southern city several years ago, a young man in the house where I was boarding received a note which ran thus: "My dear friend, I have accepted the Lord Jesus as my Saviour, and I want to join the church. Come around and tell me how to go about it." That note was sent by the manager of a great tobacco factory. On the previous Saturday evening a group of young men prayed for his conversion, and one of them said to the others, "Boys, Monday morning at ten minutes past ten o'clock I am going to our friend's office to urge him to become a Christian. Pray for me now, and pray for me at that time, that the Spirit of God may go with me." Promptly at ten minutes past ten o'clock on Monday morning the young man entered the office of the manager, and found him seated on his high stool busy with his ledger. "Can you give me five minutes this morning?" he asked. "What do you want?" was the reply. "Do you want to talk religion to me?" "Oh, never mind, you give me five minutes." "All right, go ahead. I can stand it if you can." The earnest young Christian took a little Testament from his pocket, and, opening it, placed his finger upon a verse and

"GO GLUE THYSELF"

read: "This is a faithful saying, and worthy of all acceptation, that Christ Jesus came into the world to save sinners." "Now, my friend," he continued, "we boys have been praying for you a long time, and I have come around to tell you that I am a sinner saved by Christ, and I want to see you saved also. Good morning." The manager of the tobacco factory was not happy during that day. The figures became confused before him. He said to himself, "That young man was in earnest, and I will become a Christian as I ought."

2. THE EUNUCH WAS A MAN OF HIGH POSITION.

He was a member of the cabinet of a queen. Conventionalities surrounded him and shut him off from the common people. It is easy to talk to children for whose opinion we care little, or to the tramp on the street whose rebuff will not hurt us. It is harder to go into the company of men and women who are high in social position, surrounded by the luxuries of wealth and the dignities of honor, but Philip with the Spirit of God upon him did not stand back on this account. He was as bold to speak to the treasurer of the queen as to the rabble in Samaria. The externals of worldly position did not count much with Philip; an immortal soul was everything. It is the fashion to

EVANGELISM OLD AND NEW

abuse certain wicked men in high places, but how many of us have prayed for them and talked to them about their soul's salvation?

4. THE EUNUCH WAS DOUBTLESS A MORAL MAN.

We read this between the lines. Men who are dishonest are not apt to be entrusted with funds. The fact that he went up to Jerusalem to worship, and that he was reading his Bible, is a presumption that he was a decent sort of fellow. The moral man often puts his morality between himself and God, and hides behind it when we approach him in the name of Christ. He has what he ought to retain after he becomes a Christian, for every true Christian is moral. He has what it is easy for him to substitute for Christ. Morality is a good thing in the church and out of it, and we are apt to excuse ourselves for not approaching men of good character who are not Christians because we feel that they have much in common with us. And yet morality is not salvation. It is right relation with men, but not right relation with God.

A man in Brooklyn some time ago was arrested and sent to Sing Sing. Years ago he was immoral and had been sent to the penitentiary for a long term. He took advantage of his liberty in connection with the medical department and escaped.

"GO GLUE THYSELF"

He went West, married, came to Brooklyn, and was living an honest, industrious life with his wife and baby. He was arrested and sent back to the penitentiary because, though he was all right with his wife and child and the community, he was all wrong with the State of New York. I hope the governor pardoned him. But his being all right with the community did not make him all right with the State of New York, and your being right with men does not make you right with God, though when you get right with God you are certain to get right with men. Jesus Christ died on the cross that you might be reconciled to God. Paul wrote the letter to the Romans to prove that righteousness primarily is not right-doing, but right relation, and all our right-doing is "filthy rags" until through Jesus we come into right relation with God.

Though we may honor the moral man and esteem his friendship, we should be kind enough to give him something better than his morality. There come times in one's life when morality cannot comfort. Look at that home where the only child has died. The father is a moral man. Shall I tell him now of his morality? Shall I read to him the ten commandments, and assure him that he has kept them all? It would be like piercing his soul with a dagger of cold steel. What he needs now is a sympathetic, loving, tender Saviour, One who weeps with those who weep. It is a great unkindness in Christians to leave moral men with only their morality for their comfort in sorrow.

5. THE EUNUCH WAS ALSO A RELIGIOUS MAN.

He had been up to Jerusalem to worship. He believed in God. His worship was no sham. Man is a religious animal before he becomes a Christian, and sometimes he is brim full of religious emotion. But religion does not save; it may even curse. Next to sin, religion has cursed the nations. It is the religion of China and India and Africa that Christ must overcome before He can reign in the hearts of the people. Our religious nature needs to be purified. It is a sad fact that intense religiousness often dwells in the same person with uncleanness. I was once a guest for a week in the home of the superintendent of a great lunatic asylum, and he told me that the patients who were afflicted with religious mania were the foulest persons in his institution. He could not understand why, but simply stated the fact.

The explanation, however, is simple enough. Religion with Christ in it will lift a man heavenward; religion without Christ will drag him downward. Religion is either a wing or a weight; it

"GO GLUE THYSELF"

purifies or befouls. Now when we find that a man is religious we are apt to leave him alone. Why should Philip preach Jesus to a man who has been to the temple, and is now reading the Bible? And why should I go to my friend who attends church regularly, enjoys good music, admires splendid architecture, and is at home with religious people? Ask him whether or not the blood is on the doorpost of his heart, whether he has accepted Jesus Christ as his Saviour from sin, and his reply will indicate whether you need to urge upon him the importance of personal salvation.

Some of the most religious people are offended by the cross. They like it on the top of their church steeples, but not in their lives. They admire the attributes of Jesus, but they will not stand by Calvary and weep for their sins. They are trying to save themselves by imitating a good man, while they need to "Behold the Lamb of God which taketh away the sin of the world." These most religious people are in greatest need of a Saviour, and they are the ones that need to be approached and talked with personally. They listen to the public sermon and pass its truth on to others. The Pharisees who heard Jesus were intensely religious while they were like "whited sepulchres, fair without, and within rottenness and dead men's bones."

EVANGELISM OLD AND NEW

6. THE EUNUCH MISUNDERSTOOD THE SCRIPTURES.

He was mystified as he read. Puzzling questions filled his mind. And there are not a few people to-day who refuse to accept Christ because they cannot understand all the Bible. Years ago a young man rose in a meeting and asked for prayer. I made an engagement with him for a conversation at a certain hour. Next day he came to me with a sad face, and I asked him his difficulty. "Well," he said, "I have been troubled a long time about the question as to where Cain found his wife." This young man was a student of the university, and was letting the Devil cheat him out of his soul with such quibbling. And when I answered that question, I found that there were still other questions, just as frivolous, waiting for solution. There is much about the Bible we cannot understand, even after we have accepted Christ and received spiritual discernment. There is scarcely anything we can understand until we have surrendered to Jesus. Christ is Himself the best interpreter of His Word. A man came to Mr. Moody with a long list of questions. The blunt evangelist said, "I will answer your questions to-morrow if you will promise me one thing." "What is it?" asked the man. "I will not tell you until you will promise me to do it." "Oh, well, I will try." "Give yourself to Christ," replied

"GO GLUE THYSELF."

Moody, "and then come to me with your questions." The man went to the meeting next day to tell Mr. Moody that he had taken his advice, and now he had no questions to ask. All of them had been answered by his surrender to Jesus.

CHAPTER IX.

PAUL'S CONVERSION.

One sometimes lives an age in a few minutes. Dewey lived longer in one minute at Manila than during any ten years of his previous life. At the Diet of Worms Luther lived more than a decade. There come crises in our lives upon which focalizes all the past and all the future depends. Such was the experience of Saul of Tarsus as he approached Damascus. In a short time he becomes a new man and begins a new life. The course of events in his experience may be divided into five periods, each one a dissolving view merging into the other.

THE PERIOD OF PERSECUTION.

In this there are four steps: (1) We find the young man Saul looking on at the martyrdom of Stephen, while he watches the clothes of the murderers. (2) He consented to it. "Saul was consenting unto his death." He not only stood by and watched, but he showed by his countenance that he believed in what was being done. He had given his vote against Stephen, and now he rejoices in the execution of the sentence. At first his mind was against him; now his heart opposes.

PAUL'S CONVERSION

(3) He became a persecutor. The young man who stood by while Stephen was killed, and consented to it, now goes from house to house arresting men and women and throwing them into prison. He does this according to law. He obtained his warrants from the high priest. There are some men whose consciences are satisfied when they are doing evil within the bounds of the law. Great corporations employ lawyers that they may not violate the laws of the state and bring themselves before the courts. They are not so particular about the law of God. Liquor sellers excuse themselves for engaging in their business because the law approves it. (4) He became enthusiastic. "And Saul yet breathing out threatening and slaughter against the disciples of the Lord." Murder was the very atmosphere which he breathed, and he made an atmosphere for others. Wherever he went the opponents of Christianity caught his fire, and they became enthusiastic persecutors. One strong man in a community can do much toward making an atmosphere for or against Christ, and the atmosphere has much to do with our dispositions and actions. The fiery spirit of Saul made it easy for others to persecute. And these four steps downward may be traced in most processes of degeneration. The man who continues to look on will soon begin to consent, and

EVANGELISM OLD AND NEW.

when he consents he will soon take a hand, and when he begins to take a part it will not be long before he will become an enthusiast in evil.

Saul was stricken down by a light from heaven. He fell to the earth overwhelmed by a vision of the risen Christ. His eyes were blinded by the glory of Him whom he was persecuting. When God wished to save the Ethiopian eunuch, he sent Philip to sit by him in the chariot and unfold to him the Scriptures. But there was no use in sending a man to speak to the fiery persecutor; he would have arrested him, put him in chains, and cast him into prison. God could not approach this tiger on a level. He must strike him from above. Some men will not let God deal with them until He strikes them down and lays them prostrate. They will never look up until they find themselves flat upon their backs. Captain Sigsbee, who was on the "Maine," when it was blown up, was at one time captain of the lake steamer "Blake," when he found himself in a storm drifting toward the breakers. In order to save his vessel from utter destruction, he opened a hole in the bottom and let it sink in deep water. After the storm had abated, divers were sent down, and it was found that the vessel was resting upon the sand. It was then raised and repaired. The brave captain had to sink his vessel in order to save

PAUL'S CONVERSION

it, and God is compelled to sink some men in order to save them. They will not listen while He speaks to them in whispers of love; He must thunder in tones of judgment.

God does not refuse to use lightning. Saul was struck down by light, which, after all, is God's best lightning. It is light that strikes men down to-day. The light of God's word struck Luther while he climbed Pilate's staircase upon his knees. The light of truth struck Bunyan in his house of revelry. The light of God's truth, taught him by his mother, struck down John Newton on the deck of a ship in a storm at sea. God knows how to prostrate sinners under the overwhelming power of light from heaven. In a tone of loving rebuke God asks, "Saul, Saul, why persecutest thou me?" The repetition of Saul's name carries with it deep earnestness and love. We are reminded of the words of Jesus, "Martha, Martha, thou art cumbered with much serving." In the first "Martha" there is a rebuke; in the second there is tender love. So when he said to Peter, "Simon, Simon." "Saul, Saul, is there any reason why you should be persecuting me who died for you on Calvary?" No wonder Saul fell to the ground. It was a stroke of love as well as of light. Men who resist light succumb to love.

Prostrate on the ground, Saul cried, "Who art

thou, Lord?" The question has its own answer. Saul was in doubt as to who it was who appeared to him, but he was in no doubt as to His lordship. He felt at once that the glorious being who had revealed Himself was his Master, and in this question of surprise there is a full surrender, as if to say, "Whatever else I may learn about you, I know that thou art my Lord, the Ruler of my heart and life henceforth." The reply of Jesus was, "I am Jesus whom thou persecutest. The Christians whom you are going to arrest are a part of me. They are my body."

"And, Saul, you know that it is not easy for you to act as you do; you must kick against the goads of your conscience. The memory of the shining face of the dying Stephen is another goad that pricks you and would turn you from your persecuting course." Light and love and reason have conquered, so that Paul, trembling and astonished, said, "Lord, what wilt thou have me do? I am at your bidding; from this time forth I simply receive orders and obey. I renounce the authority of the high priest and swear allegiance to thee." The Lord said unto him, "Arise, and go unto the city, and it shall be told thee what thou must do." God now turns him over to man. The one whom he was seeking to kill is to become his instructor and friend.

PAUL'S CONVERSION.

When he arose from the earth, he found that he was blind, and his atendants had to lead him. What a contrast between the manner in which He expected to enter Damascus and the manner in which he did enter it! He expected to enter with a rattling retinue; he enters it as a blind beggar. He expected to enter leading his followers; he enters led by them. He expected to enter as a terror to Christians; he enters as their friend. What a change the power of God can bring about in a few minutes! The lion becomes the lamb, the vulture the dove, the tiger has lost its ferocity, and all this has been brought about by a vision of the Christ.

In the Zoological Gardens at Philadelphia some time ago the large puma was suffering from an abscess. The keeper lanced it and relieved the animal of pain. A few days afterward on entering the house the keeper noticed that the door of the puma's cage had by some means opened, and the animal was at large. He feared that he might be attacked but, much to his surprise, the puma fell at his feet purring and showing every sign of friendliness. It just gave up to his guidance as he led it back into the cage. There was something like gratitude in the instinct of this ferocious beast, which had been relieved of pain at the hand of its kind keeper, and it was willing to acknowledge it. It was thus that Saul of Tarsus was tamed. He saw Jesus the Saviour. A view of His loving face and pierced hands took all the fierceness out of him. He was charmed into submission by the love of his Lord. Shall the wild beast in the garden at Philadelphia put the sinner to shame? Shall a panther by its instinct recognize kindness, while men refuse to be grateful for the sacrifice of Christ on the cross?

THE PERIOD OF PRAYER.

Saul was more prostrate in soul than in body. He refused to eat and drink because his mind and heart were so taken up with more important matters. That fasting was natural. He shut himself up with God. Some think it was during this period that he saw and heard things that he could not speak of. If he spoke a word to any man, it is not recorded. His dealing was with God alone, and, when God strikes us down in any way, let us take it for granted that His purpose is that He may have us alone with Himself for a while. He shut out the sun in the heavens from Paul's vision, that the Sun of Righteousness might rise within his soul. The Lord said to Ananias, "Behold, he prayeth," and when God's severe dealings lead us to pray, the blessing begins at once. It was a long way from persecuting to praying, though not

PAUL'S CONVERSION

a long time. From breathing threatenings and slaughter, Saul began to breathe the spirit of prayer.

This transformation cannot be explained on natural grounds. It is God at work. And the conversion of this persecutor should encourage us to expect the conversion of those whom we cannot approach with our words of testimony. We can simply give them over to God while we ask Him to strike them down with His light and love.

THE PERIOD OF PREPARATION.

God sends to Saul a man who has seen the Lord in a vision. Ananias said, "Brother Saul, the Lord, even Jesus, that appeared to thee in the way that thou camest, hath sent me." It is good for a young convert to meet a man with a vision. It is a blessed experience when two men who had seen visions of the Christ come together for mutual help. When the traveller in Switzerland comes to a height from which there can be seen a beautiful landscape, he finds a telescope ready for use. By the payment of a small sum his natural vision is enlarged, and he sees the beauties and sublimities of nature about him. There are men of God who are to the spiritual vision what the telescope is to the natural; they give us larger views of God's truth and ways. It is well to make any sacrifice to be in contact with them. Through this man with a vision God commissions Paul and sends him forth on his life work. "He is a chosen vessel unto me to bear my name before the Gentiles and kings and the children of Israel, and I will show him how great things he must suffer for my name's sake." The sword that has been breaking the vessels of the Lord has been transmuted into a vessel which is to carry the water of life to the uttermost parts of the earth. He who has been blaspheming my name shall now bear my name even before kings.

God puts Paul to a severe test. He appeals to the heroic in him. He does not say, "I will give you a good time; you shall be happy in your surroundings, and at last have a crown in heaven." Such treatment would have made him into a weakling. When Garibaldi was about to lead the patriotic troops of Italy to battle, he said, "Soldiers, I lead you to the bivouac, to hunger and cold, it may be to death. All that are willing to follow me, step out and stack your guns." And every man of them stepped out and stacked his gun. So Jesus says to us, "There is a great battle to be fought, and a glorious victory to be won. I offer you the cross which I myself have borne. The crown will come, but the cross is here. Will you take it and follow me?"

PAUL'S CONVERSION

In the town of Wycomb, England, there has been a custom for over two hundred years of weighing the mayor after he had been elected. It is meant to signify that the people who have exalted him to this office are weighing him mentally and morally, and that they expect him to give his full weight during his administration to everything that is good. God is weighing Paul, and tells him that he expects him to give all that he is and has to the work of carrying the gospel to the world. Paul accepts the conditions, and goes forward to the work. Brave General White was in England at one time when his regiment was sent to the front, and he requested that he might be permitted to go with them. The prime minister, however, was anxious to have his presence and advice in the perplexing situation, and he begged him to remain with them in London. General White's reply was, "Suppose my regiment should be cut to pieces, and I not with them." He could not bear the thought of his men dying for their country, while he was in a place of safety. It was not so much the fear that they might gain the victory in his absence as that they might be defeated, and he could not share the danger and disgrace with them. No wonder that the brave General won the Victoria cross. As God sent forth Paul, He sends us forth for suffering and for ser-

EVANGELISM OLD AND NEW

vice. He would not make weaklings of us by appealing to our love of ease. He would rather make heroes by placing before us dangers and difficulties.

THE PERIOD OF PREACHING AND PROVING.

"Straightway Paul preached Christ in the synagogues that He is the Son of God." He had only one message; He knew only one thing certainly. He had seen the risen Chirst, and he would proclaim Him to His enemies. There may be much profit in a long theological course in the seminary, provided it does not freeze out our spiritual life, but the young convert need not wait for a theological training to enable him to tell others of the Christ who has saved his soul from death. But Paul not only preached that Jesus Christ died; he proved it. He had only one argument, which they could not gainsay, and that was himself. "A few days ago I was a fiery persecutor; I am now a devout worshipper. Last week I hated this Christ; now I love Him better than life. Then I wanted to kill Christians; now I want to save everybody." Paul knew no other message than Jesus Christ, and no better proof of His deity than his own conversion.

CHAPTER X.

REVOLUTION AND GROWTH VS. EVOLUTION AND MAGIC.

The power of the Bible confirms the proposition that it is a revelation from God. It is the living Word. It transforms character. It makes a revolution such as no book of human authorship has ever done. Pastor Hirsch says that in his parish visitation he gave a Bible to a seller of low literature. At first she refused it, and when she consented to accept it, she said, "I will sell it." "All right," replied Mr. Hirsch, "but read it before you sell it." When he returned to that bookstore several months afterward, he found that all the low literature had been cast out. The woman, who had never read the Bible before, was so impressed by its truths, and her character was so changed, that she decided to run only a first-class bookstore. The Bible thus cleanses and keeps clean every heart and business that will accept its teachings.

WHAT A DESPISED TESTAMENT DID.

After the battle of Inkerman a dead soldier was found with his bloody finger pressed upon a leaf in his Bible. As they lifted his body, the leaf tore out and one of his comrades read aloud the words upon which his finger rested, "I am the resurrection and the life." While he was dying, he looked

EVANGELISM OLD AND NEW

through these words of God into the future bright as hope in Christ could make it. And no other book could give such an experience to a dying soldier on the battlefield. A colporter handed another Bible to a soldier in the Crimean war as the troops were leaving Toulon. He said, "I will light my pipe with it." The colporter regretted that he had given it to him, but prayed that God would somehow use it for his good. Several years afterward the colporter stopped for the night in a peasant's home in France. He saw lying on the table a well-worn, soiled Bible. On opening it he noticed that the front leaves were torn out. The mother said to him, "I prize that Bible very highly. My boy was in the Crimean war and was mortally wounded in one of the battles. It was this book that led him to Christ and gave him a hope of heaven." The colporter recognized the book as the same he had given to the soldier at Toulon. He had torn out some of the leaves to light his pipe with, yet, when the hour of suffering came, he turned for light and comfort to the book which he had despised. And what took place in these special cases is the common experience of all Christians. The Book is the voice of God, life and light and joy to everyone who believes it. It brings about a revolution through the immediate agency of God.

REVOLUTION VS. EVOLUTION

SIN REVOLUTIONARY.

Sin is revolutionary, and it does quick work. It made Cain in a few years capable of murdering his brother in a religious quarrel. It makes short work of men and families to-day. One would expect that a revolutionary force is needed to contend with sin, and such is Christianity.

GOD OF NATURE REVOLUTIONARY.

As we read the Bible we are convinced that it contains a series of revolutions. It begins in its first verse with a revolution: "In the beginning God created the heaven and the earth." Imagine, if you can, a universe with only God in it. By His word and will He brings matter into existence; a revolution truly. At the proper time this Creator produces life, which produces another revolution. Put into the ground a handful of corn, and within a few months there will be a revolution. Life makes revolution. Introduce into this vegetable life animal life, and soon there is another revolution. Now bring on the scene a man with reason, conscience, imagination and you have another revolution.

In growth there is "the blade, the ear and the full corn in the ear." That is development of the corn after its kind. Evolution demands that there shall be a transmutation from one kind to another.

EVANGELISM OLD AND NEW

Herbert Spencer begins with a single cell, and from that imagines that all the present world of vegetable, animal and human beings evolved. That is not growth, but magic, such as observation and experience do not justify in accepting. Creation was evidently a crisis with a view to a process. Such was the introduction of vegetable life, then animal, and finally of mental and moral life. And such is Christianity. In the world and in the human heart it is a crisis with a view to a process. A revolution followed by a development of life after its kind.

REVOLUTIONS IN HISTORY.

Run your mind through Biblical history and mark the periods of revolution. Certainly the flood, which destroyed the world, saving only one family, was a revolution. The destruction of Sodom and Gomorrah, with the deliverance of Lot, was a revolution. The calling of Abraham, separating him from his idolatries, and making him and his descendants the repository of truth, was another revolution. The deliverance of the Israelites from Egypt by a series of awful miracles was a revolution. The birth of Jesus Christ, begotten by the Holy Ghost of a human mother, was another revolution. And, in order to accept Christ at all, the evolutionist must deny His miraculous

REVOLUTION VS. EVOLUTION

conception. He does not allow God to come on the the scene and do as He pleases. He can have power in nature, but no power over His power. He must work in obedience to His own servants, which we call natural law. The Bible gives Him the larger liberty of working in person and performing miracles in ways that seem to us to be supernatural. The miracles of Jesus were certainly revolutionary. Nicodemus was right. "No man can do these miracles that thou doest except God be with him."

TRUTH REVOLUTIONARY.

The teachings of Jesus as you will see by reading the first ten verses of the Sermon on the Mount were revolutionary. They did not grow out of His time. "Never man spake like this man." The death of Jesus was revolutionary. No founder of any other religion ever dreamed of dying for his followers. Buddha shunned death until he reached the age of eighty, and then he died because he must. Confucius and Zoroaster did not conceive of the idea of sacrificing themselves for the good of others. Mohammed established his religion by killing rather than being killed. "For myself," says Max Muller, "I claim that in the discharge of my duties for about forty years, I have devoted as much time as any man living to

EVANGELISM OLD AND NEW

the study of these sacred books, and the one reference which you will find through all of them is salvation by works. They all say that salvation must be purchased, must be bought with a price, but the sole price, the sole purchase money, must be by our own work and deservings." Jesus only died to save a lost world. He is the author of salvation by grace. No wonder the sun darkened, the rocks rent, and the dead were raised during the tragedy of the crucifixion, for the death of Christ was the beginning of such a revolution in the world as had never been seen before. By this death He is to take the human heart by storm; its appeal to gratitude and love cannot be resisted. "And I, if I be lifted up from the earth, will draw all men unto me." The malefactor by His side is swept by the force of this revolution into the kingdom of God. A new force is now at work in the world. Dying for others is to take the place of making others die for us.

THE RESURRECTION AND PENTECOST.

The resurrection of Jesus was certainly a revolution, and the evolutionists, in order to explain it away, must talk a good deal of nonsense about "suspended animation" and what not. He was killed, pronounced dead by friend and enemy, buried, and on the third day rose from the dead.

REVOLUTION VS. EVOLUTION

The bloody water brought from His side by the Roman spear was the credential of His death; His living and eating with His disciples for forty days was the credential of His resurrection. This cannot be explained on any theory of growth from within; it was effected by the power of Almighty God. The ascension from the top of Olivet was a revolution, and the man in white spoke to the disciples of a revolution like it when He shall come "in power and great glory." Pentecost was a revolution. After you have read Canon Farrar's "Early Days of Christianity" you must be convinced that in the corruption of the pagan world and the formalism of the Jewish world, there was nothing out of which the Christian church could be evolved. Among the pagans vice was virtue. as the unearthing of Pompeii suggests, and among the Pharisees, who were the best of the Jews, hypocrisy and formalism prevailed. And yet, in one day, through the descent of the Spirit, showing Himself as a tongue of fire and rushing mighty wind, three thousand people were transformed into Christians; no gradual growth from within, but the descent of the Spirit upon them brought about this change.

PAUL'S CONVERSION.

Paul's conversion was a revolution. On his way to Damascus with warrants in his pocket to arrest

EVANGELISM OLD AND NEW

Christians, breathing out threatenings against the church, full of hatred and murder, he hears a voice from heaven and sees a light brighter than the noonday sun. The cruel persecutor is suddenly transformed into an humble inquirer. "Lord, what wilt thou have me to do?" Within a few days this Paul is upholding what he tried to destroy, and suffering the loss of all things. He gives the remainder of his life to heroic service in the cause of Christ. Such is Christianity in the world and in the human heart. It brings about a revolution through the immediate agency of God. It introduces a new life, which grows and develops after its kind. The first birth is not the germ out of which the second birth grows. We become partakers of the divine nature; it is God in the soul making all things new.

FAILURES OF CULTURE.

The attempt to make men Christians by the process of education has been tried with dismal failure. Bishop Colenso took a band of Zulu youths and gave them a good education in England. After they had advanced in their studies, he suggested that they now turn their attention to the consideration of the claims of Christianity, but, in the words of Dr. Gordon, "They kicked up their heels and went back to their former heathen prac-

REVOLUTION VS. EVOLUTION

tices." The good bishop had to confess that his experiment was a failure. Hans Egede spent fifteen years in Greenland educating the people, attempting, as he said, to bring them to a place where they could become intelligent Christians. With a broken heart he preached his farewell sermon from the text, "I have labored in vain; I have spent my strength for naught." Two years later John Beck succeeded Egede on this field. He began at once to preach Christ crucified, and the result was the conversion of Kajarnack, who became a flame of evangelistic zeal amid the frozen regions of Greenland. Christ's death and resurrection in their revolutionary power effected in him at once what fifteen years of training could not accomplish in others. Robert Moffat was told that if he went to preach to Africaner, the cruel chief would make out of his skull a drinking-cup and use his skin for a drumhead. But Moffat, trusting in God, went to Africaner, and told him the story of the suffering Christ and the risen Lord. The result was that the lion became a lamb; the cruel chieftain was transformed into an earnest Christian, so that Moffat, after years of association with him, wrote this testimony of his Christianity: "I do not once remember having occasion to be grieved with him or to complain of any part of his conduct." Nothing short of the revolutionary power of the gospel can explain the experience of Paul, Kajarnack, Africaner, John Newton, Jerry McAulay, and scores of others who have been won immediately and directly from lives of wickedness to lives of righteousness.

Such has been the effect of Biblical teachings in many communities. James Calvert tells us that when he arrived at the Fiji Islands, the first thing he had to do was to gather up the bones and flesh which had been left over from a cannibal feast the day before. Within less than half a century, which is scarcely a speck of time in the cycle of evolution, these men, once cannibals, were sitting at the table of the Lord. The death of Christ, revealed in the Bible and symbolized by the broken bread and the pouring wine, had wrought this revolution. On the island of Aneityum is the monument of John Geddie, bearing this inscription: "When he landed in 1848 there were no Christians; when he left in 1872, there were no heathen."

DARWIN A WITNESS.

Some of us have heard from the lips of John G. Paton how the whole island of Aniwa has been turned to Christ, so that among all its inhabitants there is not a single heathen. When Mr. Darwin

REVOLUTION VS. EVOLUTION

visited Terra Del Fuega, in 1833, he wrote: "The Fuegians are in a more miserable state of barbarism than I ever expected to have seen any human being." He thought it would be impossible to civilize them. On his second visit in 1869 he was astonished to find that these people, whom he had regarded as below the domestic animals, had been transformed into Christian men and women. In his astonishment he wrote: "I certainly should have predicted that not all the missionaries in the world could have done what has been done. It is wonderful and it shames me, as I have always prophesied a failure. It is a grand success." In a letter to the London Missionary Society, enclosing twenty-five pounds for the work, Mr. Darwin said: "I shall feel proud if your committee shall think fit to elect me as honorary member of your society." It is evident that Darwin perceived that a revolutionary, rather than an evolutionary force had been at work on Terra Del Fuega.

Such is the Bible, because the living God goes with it and works as He will. On any day in Spring one may see in Greenwood Cemetery abundant life clothing the hills into beauty of shrub and grass and flowers, but underneath the granite and marble shafts there is no appearance of life. Death is revolutionary. It soon destroys feature and form, and reduces our friends to dust. If evolution were my hope, I should stand in Greenwood full of despair. But I believe in the God of revolution. "In a moment, in the twinkling of an eye, at the last trumpet the dead shall be raised." From underneath those heavy shafts shall come forth the bodies of our loved ones, glorified and immortal. Let us urge our friends to believe in the Lord Jesus Christ, "who saves" in a moment, "in the twinkling of an eye," and gives the spiritual life that grows stronger day by day.

CHAPTER XI.

SOUL-WINNING.

Solomon wrote in Prov. 11:30: "The fruit of righteousness is a tree of life, and he that winneth souls is wise."

Fruit usually grows upon trees. But in this Scripture fruit is the tree. Let Psalm 1:3 shine upon it, and its meaning is plain: "He shall be like a tree planted by the rivers of water." Every Christian is a tree, and his best fruit is another tree like himself. "The good seed are the children of the kingdom." The business of the Christian is to make others Christian.

Soul-winning is the alphabet of the Christian spirit. The new-born soul desires to win another to Christ. What the alphabet is to literature this soul-winning spirit is to Christianity. Shakespeare, with all his wide range of thought, does not get beyond the alphabet. And building Christian character or a church without the soul-winning spirit is like writing "Hamlet" without the alphabet.

Therefore, "He that winneth souls is wise." It requires wisdom, and it is the part of wisdom to do it. The wisdom that would promote the building of Christian character can do it in no better way. Soul-winning strengthens faith, brightens

EVANGELISM OLD AND NEW

hope, fosters humility, cultivates patience and increases love. If wisdom would make us happy, there is no joy like it outside of heaven. If wisdom would enrich us for eternity, this is the best way to lay up treasures where "neither moth nor rust doth corrupt." If wisdom would seek glory that fades not away, "They that be wise shall shine as the firmament, and they that turn many to righteousness as the stars forever and ever." If you would obey him who is the wisdom of God, you must win souls, for the first command to His disciples was, "Follow me, and I will make you to become fishers of men." His last command was simply an expansion of the first, "Go ye into all the world and preach the gospel to every creature."

EVANGELICAL AND EVANGELISTIC.

Between these two commands are the words: "The Son of man is come to seek and to save that which was lost." "What man of you, having an hundred sheep, if he lose one of them, doth not leave the ninety and nine in the wilderness and go after that which is lost until he find it?" That is to say, the alpha and omega of Christianity is soul-winning; and every letter between the first and the last should be permeated by the spirit which seeks the lost. It is not enough to be evangelical. We must be evangelistic. The evangelical church is a

SOUL-WINNING

reservoir of pure water without a pipe running anywhere. If you will take the trouble to go to it and climb the embankment, you will get a good drink. The evangelistic church is a reservoir of pure water with a pipe to every heart in the community and every nation in the world.

Evangelical may mean truth on ice; evangelistic means truth on fire. Evangelical may mean a bomb-proof for defense; evangelistic means an army on the march with every face toward the foe. Evangelical sings, "Hold the fort, for I am coming;" evangelistic sings, "Storm the fort, for God is leading." The need of the church is not evangelicalism as a thing to fight for, but evangelism as a force to fight with. The evangelical creed merely held and defended becomes a fossil, only a thing of interest; but the evangelistic life which feeds upon evangelical truth is a force against which the gates of hell cannot prevail. An evangelical may be a mere formalist, and there is no recognition of him in the New Testament, except as he is rebuked; but a New Testament evangelist is a man full of the life of God, and making alive those to whom he ministers.

1. THE MEANING.

Let us now consider this all important subject of soul-winning in four aspects:

EVANGELISM OLD AND NEW

What is it to win a soul? It is certainly more than inducing a person to join a church. That is important. There are too many believers who attend churches and refuse to become an organic part of any one. They are spiritual pleasure seekers. They look at the paper and go where the subject or the music seems most attractive. At best they are only "bush-whackers," and ought somehow to be pressed into the regular army. "One shall chase a thousand, and two put ten thousand to flight;" that is, two together are ten times stronger than one alone. Organization multiplies your influence by ten. You have no right, therefore, to remain outside the organized church of Christ. But one can join the church, be baptized and partake of the Lord's Supper without being a Christian. We may make our churches so worldly in spirit that wordly people will feel perfectly at home as members of them. They become adherents; and adherents, you know, are barnacles which help to sink the ship. The real convert has become a "partaker of the divine nature." (II. Peter 1:4). He has been "born from above." (John 3:3). There will be conviction of sin. Sinai must strike with its lightning before Calvary will glow with its light. "The sharp needle of the law must pierce the soul before it will receive the silken thread of the gospel." The patient must

SOUL-WINNING

realize that he is sick before he will take the physician's medicine. Every one must see his guilt before he will cry for pardon.

CONVICTION OF SIN.

Be greatly encouraged, therefore, in trying to win a soul to Christ when you find that he is burdened with a sense of guilt. Do not try to easily dispel it. I heard of a dilettanti preacher delivering a sermon on the new birth. After the sermon a man came up to him and said that he was greatly troubled, for he was certain that he had not been born again. "Oh," said the preacher, "I am sorry if I made you feel uncomfortable. I did not so intend it." "But," said the anxious inquirer, "I have not been born again, and you said that one must be." "Do not be troubled about that," continued the preacher, "Do your duty, be honest and upright as you have been and you will be all right." Now that preacher was guilty of murder. Not the murder of the body, but, what is infinitely worse, the murder of the soul. Why did he not point to the Lamb of God, and thus let the burdened heart find rest by believing in Him who bore the guilt and washes away the stain of sin? Trouble on account of sin, however, is not enough. "As many as received Him, to them gave He power to become the sons of God, even to them that believed on His name." (John 1:12). There must be acceptance of Jesus Christ. Even turning from sin is not sufficient. God did not tell the bitten Israelites simply to look away from the bite of the serpent, but to look to the serpent of brass uplifted in the camp. Reformation is simply turning from sin; regeneration is turning from sin unto Christ. To reform is to remain deformed; to be born again by faith in the uplifted Jesus is to take into our hearts the life that will sooner or later make us absolutely like Him. When a man confesses that he has sinned and is sorry for it, and tells you that he has accepted Jesus Christ as Saviour, you may then rejoice that you have won a soul for earth and heaven.

2. THE MEANS.

The Word of God is the instrument. "Born again, not of corruptible seed but of incorruptible, by the Word of God." (I. Pet. 1:23). You can bring people to the church, to a creed, to yourself, by your own words; but if you would win them to Christ, use the God-breathed words of Scripture. Arm yourself with the best texts. If you meet an anxious inquirer, say to him, "He that believeth on the Son hath everlasting life." (John 3:36). When you find a man who thinks that he is too

SOUL-WINNING

bad to be saved, give to him the words, "Him that cometh unto me I will in no wise cast out." (John 6:37). When you find one troubled like the jailer under deep conviction of sin, say to him, "Believe on the Lord Jesus Christ and thou shalt be saved." (Acts 16:31). Let there be no philosophizing. Do not argue. Simply proclaim the glad tidings. A doctor need not give to the patient a chemical analysis of the medicine he prescribes. The baker need not talk to a hungry man about the constituents of bread. Let him give the loaf that will satisfy hunger. If you find a sad heart who believes that he is not one of the elect, speak to him lovingly of the last great promise of the Bible, "Whosoever will, let him take of the water of life freely." (Rev. 22:17). Fill the quiver of your memory with these arrows of truth, and trust the strong bow of the Spirit to send them to the mark. Never stir up controversy; keep to the Word of God, and it will be the sword to pierce where piercing is needed, and the balm of Gilead where healing is needed.

THE AGENT.

A Christian is the agent. Sometimes bad men in the ministry have preached the Word of God and sinners have been converted. God may honor

EVANGELISM OLD AND NEW

His own Word even should the Devil proclaim it, specially when earnest, sincere Christians are praying for His blessing upon it. But the Christian himself, redeemed by Christ, is the one who can best recommend Christ to others. If you would be a soul-winner, therefore, you must be a righteous man—righteous in the sense that you are in right relation to your fellow-men, and therefore have influence. Influence without power can do little; power without influence is hindered. All your influence, mental, moral, social and financial, ought to be laid on the altar of Christ.

But even good influence will not of itself win a soul. God must give the new heart. We are "created in Christ Jesus unto good works." (Eph. 2:10). Only the Creator can make a new creation. A soul-winner must, therefore, walk with God, keeping in touch with His mighty power. Mr. Spurgeon tells how Dickens was kept from becoming a spiritualist. He went to a seance, and asked for the spirit of Lindley Murray. When the spirit in due time appeared, Dickens inquired, "Are you Lindley Murray?" The spirit replied, "I are." Dickens knew at once that it was a fraud, for Lindley Murray would have used good grammar. The soul-winner must impress sinners with the fact that he is genuine, that there is no sham about him or his religion.

SOUL-WINNING

FULL ASSURANCE.

In order that one may be a successful soul-winner, he must have full assurance of his own salvation. To pull others out of the flood one needs to have a good footing. Nothing convicts like conviction. Faith produces faith. Doubt as to the inspiration of the Bible or the deity of Christ paralyzes. You are in a poor condition to point others to Christ if you are not certain that Christ has saved you. You would be a poor agent for an Atlantic steamship line if you had a doubt as to the safety of the vessels; and yet men have won others to Christ when they themselves were not sure of salvation. Bunyan declares that he preached as a criminal to criminals, standing in chains before a people in chains. But he believed that God could save sinners, and, though he felt that he himself was not saved, he would recommend the Saviour to others. While you would not stop Bunyan from preaching, by all means trust the Word of God, and thus be sure of your own salvation, that you may speak what you know and testify to what you have seen.

EVEN LITTLE CHILDREN.

People of all ages and culture may succeed in winning souls to Christ. Little children have been successful soul-winners. In the town of Stroudsburg, Pa., a little girl attended a revival service and gave her heart to Jesus. She went home and asked her worldly mother if she might join the church, and her mother would not consent. The child said, "The preacher told me I must accept Jesus; and if I accept Jesus I am a Christian and ought to join the church." She lovingly persisted until the mother finally consented to let the child unite with the church. "And now," said the little girl, "would it look well for me to join the church while mother stays away? Won't you accept Jesus? Then you, too, will be a Christian." The mother and child knelt together and the mother surrendered herself to the Lord. That evening both mother and child persuaded the father to go to church, and the next Sunday the whole family stood up and confessed Jesus. "A little child shall lead them."

A Sunday school teacher in winning a boy or girl to Christ may be bringing into the kingdom a whole family. I heard the other day of a blatant infidel in a small town who began to go to church. The pastor was surprised, and an evangelist, who was conducting the meeting, learned from the man the reason for his coming. The man said, "Yes, I am an infidel, as you call it; but you have taken a flank movement on me. You have converted my child, and that is an argument I cannot answer."

SOUL-WINNING

Through the conversion of his child the bold infidel became an humble Christian.

ALL SORTS OF PEOPLE.

God needs all sorts of people as soul-winners. Where one fails another will succeed. It took four men to bring one paralytic to Christ.

Several miles above Milton, Pa., when the ice was breaking up, a farmer got into one of his boats purposing to pull it out of the river. A floating mass of ice struck it, breaking it loose from the bank, and carrying it and him out into the current. A neighbor, seeing the danger, mounted a horse and with all speed rode down to Milton. The people of the town gathered all the ropes they could secure, went out on the bridge, and suspended a line of dangling ropes from the bridge across the river. They could not tell at just what point the boat with the farmer would pass under, so they put a rope down every two or three feet clear across. Bye and bye the farmer was seen, wet and cold, standing in the boat half full of water, drifting down the rapid current. When he saw the ropes dangling within reach, he seized the nearest one, was drawn up and saved. Now one rope might not have answered the purpose. The pastor hangs the rope of salvation from the pulpit, and no one present seems to get near it, but if every Christian in the community will assist in hanging out the ropes, sinners in the currents of destruction will certainly be saved.

3. THE METHOD.

Preachers should expect God to save someone every time they preach. Spurgeon never preached a sermon that did not have in it the way of life, and this is the secret of his great success. In every audience there are apt to be some who are seeking salvation, and to ignore the inquirer while we edify the Christian is like giving food to the well-fed while we overlook the starving.

THE SUNDAY MORNING SERMON.

Pastors need to remember that God is as willing to save on Sunday morning as on Sunday evening. Though the message of the morning should be for Christians, the sermon should have in it something for the indifferent business man who never goes to church on Sunday evening, and something for the stranger—a stranger also to Christ—who expects to attend another church, if not a place of amusement, in the evening. A few conversions on Sunday morning would do more to edify and inspire Christians than ever so many sermons on growing in grace. If we expect conversions, we shall not be disappointed. Some time ago earnest souls in the Ruggles Street

SOUL-WINNING

Church of Boston began to pray for conversions in the morning, and it made me careful to make clear in every sermon the way of life. After the benediction one Sunday morning I heard the unusual sound of sobbing, and, on looking in the direction of it, I saw a young woman sitting in the front seat with her face in her hands, weeping as with a broken heart. A lady near me said, "That young woman is hysterical." I found, however, that it was not hysterics, but genuine conviction of sin. When I asked her what troubled her, she replied in a tone I shall not soon forget, "Oh, pastor, my heart aches so I feel that I cannot go home without relief." My associate pastor, whose passion is personal work, went with her into the study, and in about twenty minutes she came out with a radiant face which left no doubt as to the genuineness of her joy. As she walked down the isle, she met a young lady friend, who, not finding her at home had returned to the church in search of her. She told her friend that she had just accepted Christ and was very happy. My associate pastor spoke a few words to her friend, and she, too, kneeling beside them in the isle, quietly accepted Jesus. That evening I saw one of these young women in the aftermeeting trying to lead others into the light and joy she had received through Christ.

EVANGELISM OLD AND NEW

Another Sunday morning as I closed my sermon I felt impressed that the Spirit was moving upon the people with unusual power, and I did what I had never done in Boston before, asked all who had not confessed Christ as Saviour and Lord to come forward during the singing. The first one who came was a man over fifty years of age; the next a lady over seventy, then young men and women, until fourteen were seated in the front pews. It was a melting time. Those who had been praying for conversions on Sunday mornings wept tears of joy. I believe there was more power in those fourteen quiet testimonies for Christ than in my sermon. Indeed, I have forgotten the subject of the sermon, and the feature of that morning's service which stands out most prominently in the minds of the people is the fact that fourteen new converts gave testimony for Christ.

FEEDING AND FISHING.

Oh for fire from God that will melt the conventionalism of our morning service and bring glory to Christ in salvation, as well as in edification! There is a demand on the part of mature Christians that pastors should feed the sheep; and the sheep need to be fed. But why should sheep depend altogether on the cut-feed the pastor brings them

SOUL-WINNING

on Sunday morning? They have in their Bibles the green pastures into which they can go and graze for themselves. A dear old deacon in a former pastorate came to me after the evening sermon, and said significantly, "Pastor, feed the sheep, feed the sheep." I thought I knew him well enough to say, "I have fed you dear old sheep now until you are so fat you can hardly walk, and I wish you would move around and work off some of your superfluous flesh in seeking to bring others into the fold." If I mistake not, he smiled rather sadly; but I fear he continued to believe that if the pastor fed well the ninety and nine, the one that was lost would somehow get back into the sheepfold.

The command to feed the sheep does not abrogate the command to fish for men, and the word "feed" should be kept out of the command to fish. It is not our mission to feed fish, that is, to cultivate the natural man until he has so greatly improved that he may be labeled a Christian. The fish that live in the lower realm of darkness, grub and gravel, must be transformed by the new birth into sheep fitted for the higher realm of landscape, sun and sky. The Babel process of reaching heaven by building up from beneath is not the New Testament method. "Ye must be born from above." George Whitefield preached over three hundred times from that text, and when asked why he preached so often from the same text replied, "Because ye must be born again."

The pagan theory of evolution from beneath has in many places displaced the Christian teaching of revolution by the introduction of life from above. The philosophical talk about saving a man one hundred years before he is born would leave Saul of Tarsus to go on to Damascus and down to hell, but God can save the persecutor like a lightning flash by entering into his heart, transforming him into a devout worshipper and a courageous missionary. There is something in heredity, but it is not something that saves. It is the new heredity that makes us "partakers of the divine nature." Christ can enter the heart of the vilest and make them sons of God. The need of the day is re-emphasis of sudden, instantaneous conversion, a crisis with a view to the process of growth. There is no growing into it, but there is immense growth in it. The Spirit wrote to a pastor, "Do the work of an evangelist," as if He would warn against the temptation of the pastor to be content with simply feeding the sheep. Let us seek for our audiences the sheep-nature, and then they will have a taste for the sheep-food we bring them. The new birth is certainly the imparting of the new taste. "If so be ye have tasted that the Lord is gracious."

SOUL-WINNING

(I. Peter 11:3). And until this new taste is given, the people are not ready for spiritual food.

PERSONAL WORK.

Public preaching, however, is no substitute for face to face conversation. Jesus sets us the example of personal work. One sentence spoken in loving earnestness to the individual may do more than ten sermons delivered to the crowd. One afternoon as I was on my way to a meeting, which was one of what we were trying to make a revival series, I felt a trifle discouraged because no unsaved people were coming to the church. I was compelled to preach every day to a small number of "regulars." I knew who would be there before I went. They were the "Tenth Legion," the old Guard, who are a constant source of encouragement to a pastor and yet a source also of discouragement. He could not do without them, and sometimes he hardly knows what to do with them. They go to church and receive with appreciation everything that he gives them. They are good conservative people who are going to heaven, but they do not seem to be taking others with them. I knew that this small company of faithful people would be there ready for my message, but the burden of my soul was for the unsaved who were not

EVANGELISM OLD AND NEW

coming. Looking just ahead of me I saw three young men standing on the street corner talking pleasantly with each other, and the thought came, "Why not try to win these young men to Christ? He can save on the street as well as in the church." So I walked up to them and asked in as cheerful a voice as I could command, "Young gentlemen, are you all Christians?" "Yes, thank you," replied two of them, "we are members of the Methodist church." "No," answered the third with rather an embarrassed expression. "I am not, but my mother is a member of the same church with these young men." I said to him, "Will you not come with me to a meeting we are to hold in a few minutes?" "Thank you," he replied, "but I haven't time, for I am very busy preparing for examinations in High School next week." The Spirit seemed to give me the right answer when I asked the question, "Are you ready for the great examination in the future?" and I passed on to the meeting. Within a few minutes I saw the young man come in at the door and take a back seat. He is now a minister of the gospel, and says that his Christian life began on the street corner when the question was asked which he could not answer until he had accepted Jesus Christ as Saviour. It is no exaggeration, I think, to say that God did more through me in that three minutes' conversa-

SOUL-WINNING

tion on the street corner than by any ten sermons
I preached during the series of meetings.

HOW A SALOONKEEPER WAS CONVERTED.

A saloonkeeper's wife attended our church in
Baltimore, and was happily converted. The husband at home saw the change in her, and, loving
her as he did, was troubled about his own soul, although he tried to hide it by frivolous conversation. The wife said she believed that he would be
converted if I would go to the saloon and speak to
him face to face. I went and met him in a back
room. We talked for half an hour, and I told him
all the bad things I could think of about the saloon
business, asking him to give it up for his wife's
sake and become a Christian. He had been a
member of the Episcopal church years ago, and
seemed sorry that he had to sell liquor to make a
living. On rising to leave, I asked him if he would
pray with me. "I have no objection," he replied,
and we knelt side by side. I began my prayer
very much in the spirit of my conversation, which
was not as loving and tender as it might have
been; "Oh, Lord, bless my friend here, and help
him to give up his miserable business—a business
that has done more harm that all the other evil
forces in this community." Thinking that I meant
for him to say a prayer with me after the Episcopal

EVANGELISM OLD AND NEW

style, he began right after me: "Oh, Lord, bless my friend here and help him to give up his miserable business." In his mouth, you see, it meant me, and I felt a trifle embarrassed. I tried to shape my prayer so as not to ricochet quite so much, and he, feeling the embarrassment also, dropped out; but I did not utter another word of criticism. My heart grew tender and warm toward him. As he followed me to the door, I saw that he was convulsed with laughter, and I might have felt like joining him, if I had not thought of the wife whose disappointment over the failure of my visit would be so great.

I left the door sick at heart, fearing that all serious impressions had been dissipated by the ludicrous double prayer. But I continued to pray that God would overrule all and save that man. Others prayed for him with me. Two or three years after this I preached in Baltimore, and, as I came down the pulpit steps after the sermon, a man met me with a cordial hand grasp saying, "Do you know me?" But I could not recognize him until he asked: "Do you remember that prayer in the back room of a saloon?" "Yes," I said, "I shall never forget that." "Well," he continued, "I am that man, and I thought it would interest you to know that wife and I are members of this church. We run the gospel wagon and preach every day."

SOUL-WINNING

"Tell me about your conversion," I said. "Well," he went on to say, "when you left the saloon I went behind the bar and had many a hearty laugh during the day at your expense, but I could not rest at night for my conscience was hurting me. So I said one morning to my wife, 'If you say so, we will go out of this business though we starve.' She was willing, and kneeling by her side I accepted Jesus Christ as my Saviour."

SUCCESSFUL FAILURES.

I have told this story, which does not reflect any credit, because it illustrates the fact that God can use awkward efforts in doing personal work. You feel that you cannot succeed because you lack fitness. You do not know how to approach people. No matter, go about it at once, and if you feel, as I did, that you have failed, God can turn your very failure into ultimate success. The fact is, you will never feel specially fitted for it. Such work makes one conscious of helplessness as nothing else does. It throws him back upon God for guidance and strength every moment. Self-sufficiency would doom you to failure, while self-distrust linked with faith in God insures success. Our sufficiency is of God, and if you place yourself at His disposal for this work, you will have cause constantly to praise Him for the manifestation of His power. No Christian can afford not to be a soul-winner, if he seeks for himself the best development, and if, what is better, he seeks the coming of Christ's kingdom in the world.

4. THE MOTIVE.

Love of souls should incite us to this glorious service. Parents who love their children should be prompted by that love to win them to Christ. Better make them Christians than leave them millionaires. If the hope of reward can influence you, there is no brighter crown awaiting the Christian than that which sparkles with the gems of souls saved through his agency. Paul looked upon the Thessalonians as his glory and crown of rejoicing at the appearing of Christ. But the brightest motive is given in the words, "The love of Christ constraineth us." (II. Cor. 5:14). Jesus came to seek and to save the lost. Nothing glorifies Him so much as the salvation of a soul. The soul-winner, therefore, spends his life adding glory to glory.

CHAPTER XII.

IN THE CITY.

Christ sent forth His disciples "two by two" into every city. The evangelization of the world was begun at Pentecost in a great city. The cities evangelized mean the world evangelized.

To-day, as in the day of Paul, the strongest enemies of the cross of Christ are in the great cities. The Word of God is light at war with darkness, health contending with disease, life in conflict with death. The man who preaches faithfully the message of God must expect to "fight the good fight of faith."

There were some in Ephesus who did not believe in "the way." The way which Paul preached was "repentance toward God and faith in our Lord Jesus Christ." It was the simple gospel of the grace of God. His purpose was to bring men into right relations with God through Christ, that they might thus be brought into right relations with each other. Some religious people in the synagogue spoke evil of "the way;" they did not believe in this simple gospel method. In their judgment there were other ways better, or just as good. They might have suggested a course of lectures in which the gospel was not to be prominent. Taking the people by guile was to them the wisest method. Paul, however, insisted on "the way," and persisted along that line.

IMITATORS.

There was at Ephesus a band of Jews under one Sceva, a renegade chief priest, who had come to Ephesus to make money by pretending to cast out evil spirits. As soon as they saw that the name of Jesus had a magic power, they decided to appropriate and use it. Their formula was, "I adjure you by Jesus Christ whom Paul preacheth." They bear good testimony to Paul when they tell us that he preached Jesus. It is preaching Jesus that makes a stir. The bad men who were possessed of devils, however, had no sympathy with these imitators. "Jesus I know, and Paul I know, but who are you?" was the reply. Imitators are to-day in the way of the gospel's success.

Some of these imitators were very zealous in making and circulating bad books, books which described their occult arts and gave them standing with the people. But the power of the gospel was so great that the owners of these books were converted, and in the streets of Ephesus there was a bonfire which must have delighted the heart of every small boy in town. Twenty thousand dollars' worth of books were placed in a pile and

IN THE CITY

burned to ashes. Such a cleansing of the literary atmosphere in our cities is greatly needed, and Paul's method of doing it is the best. He would not issue a law against free speech, but he would say, "Be so full of the Spirit and preach the gospel with such power, that editors and authors shall be converted, and made to burn up their evil publications." Paul was himself so full of the Spirit that everything about him was saturated with power; the handkerchiefs that touched his person carried with them virtue. And if the preachers and churches of our cities were thus charged with almighty power, the men who flood our streets and fill our bookstalls with vile publications would be convicted of their sins.

BAD BUSINESS.

In Ephesus was the great temple of Diana, and there were some who made their living by manufacturing and selling images of this popular goddess. The success of Paul's preaching turned away many from purchasing these wares. The result was a commotion among the craftsmen. Demetrius, doubtless President of the Association of Idol Makers, called a mass meeting and protested that this crusade against their business should stop, and he made appeal for the honor of Diana. Not only

EVANGELISM OLD AND NEW

their trade was in danger, but the glory of the goddess of Ephesus was beginning to fade.

In our cities to-day there are many lines of business and pleasure which would be overthrown by the success of the gospel. The temple of Diana in America is the liquor traffic. It is a trade in human homes and hearts and happiness. The goddess of this country, you know, is liberty, and those who make their money out of this traffic plead for the honor of their goddess. They claim that they should have the liberty to destroy their neighbors. The cry of these craftsmen and their sympathizers is "Great is the goddess of liberty which allows men to slay their fellows." Another temple of Diana is the theatre. The stage as an institution is corrupt and corrupting. Even the daily papers are now crying out against the moral filth which is poured out every day and night upon the people of our great cities. The bulletin boards are displays of spectacular obscenity.

The social wine glass is again finding its way into Christian homes. The round dance is a sort of juggernaut crushing modesty and purity beneath its wheels and leaving hundreds of wretched victims in its wake. Gambling prevails in the policy shop, at the faro table, at the race track, and around the table of the progressive euchre party. These temples of Diana stand by the sufferance of

IN THE CITY

many good people and by the open advocacy of every Demetrius who can make financial or social capital out of them.

THE SECRET OF VICTORY.

Now the important question is, How can we prevail against these evils? The answer is in Acts 19:20: "So mightily grew the Word of God and prevailed." Where the Word of God is preached in the power of the Spirit, it cannot fail to conquer. But under what conditions will it prevail? We have but to study the context in this chapter in order that we may learn.

The little church at Ephesus had not so much as heard of the Holy Spirit. These men were saved because they had accepted Jesus, but they were powerless because they had not received the Holy Spirit. They needed the tongue of fire. The first thing, therefore, which Paul did at Ephesus was to seek the enduement of power for this little band of Christians.

COMBUSTION, NOT EXPLOSION.

This was the method pursued before Pentecost. The disciples met in the upper room and continued to pray for the fulfilment of the promise of the Spirit's coming. The church within the church who believe in prayer are the tinder ready to re-

EVANGELISM OLD AND NEW

ceive the fire of the Holy Spirit. A revival is not an explosion, but a combustion. As a result of this, the tongues of the little church were all untied. Everyone was a preacher of the good tidings. There are orders in the church which ought not to be ignored, but in the matter of soul-winning we need to forget the distinction between clergy and laity, while we seek to bring men to a saving knowledge of Jesus Christ.

Paul's next step was to preach continuously for three months in the synagogue. He spoke boldly, "reasoning and persuading as to the things concerning the kingdom of God." In the synagogue was the most religious body to be found. Next to the little church that Apollos had gathered those who attended the synagogue were the best material upon which to work. It is true that they were formal, cold, lifeless, but when the little church full of power was brought among them their formality vanished, their coldness was melted, and many of them were quickened into spiritual activity. Let a small band of earnest Christians in a large church become full of the Holy Spirit and they will soon impart their fervor to the rest of the membership.

Paul's third step was to hold a protracted meeting every day for over two years. "He disputed daily in the school of one Tyrannus." Who Tyrannus was I do not know; doubtless a popular

IN THE CITY

teacher of rhetoric with a large hall in the center of Ephesus. In this hall Paul preached every day until "all that dwelt in Asia heard the word of the Lord Jesus, both Jews and Greeks."

A careful study of all great revivals will prove that they were begun and carried on in this apostolic fashion. Begin with Pentecost; first, a little company gathered around Christ, who teaches them for two or three years, then a larger company in the upper room praying and waiting, and then the great crowd, of whom three thousand were converted in one day. The revival under Wesley and Whitefield was carried on after the same fashion. First, a little band of students, the "Holy Club," at Oxford, then a larger number in the Foundry of London, and then the great throngs at Smithfield. Thus McAll's work was begun and carried on in Paris. At first, only he and his wife on fire with the Holy Spirit, then the larger number gathered around them, and finally more than one hundred secular halls in which the gospel is preached every day.

If you were commissioned to burn up a city, you would not try to set fire first to a safe deposit vault, but you would look for a more combustible building. If we are to have a genuine revival, the fire must begin in the hearts of the few who believe in Christ and the Holy Spirit.

EVANGELISM OLD AND NEW

THE BASIS OF UNITY.

Evangelism we believe to be the true basis of church unity. Whatever be our views of baptism, the Lord's Supper, and church government, we can join heart and hand with all lovers of our Lord in seeking and saving the lost. There is need in great cities of large evangelistic meetings, not only for the sake of reaching the unchurched, but for the sake of making an atmosphere for Christ.

A man who owned six saloons came to Cooper Union in New York to hear the Countess Schimmermann tell the story of Jesus and His love. At the close of the meeting he confessed Christ as his Lord, and expressed his determination to give up his business at whatever cost. The problem of the drink traffic was thus settled so far as he was concerned.

We might run through the whole list of evils, and prove that every problem can be settled by the acceptance of Jesus Christ. By the power of His sacrifice He wins our love and gives us grace to love our neighbors as ourselves, and when a man loves God and his neighbor he is a fit citizen for earth and heaven.

CHAPTER XIII.
IN THE OPEN AIR.

We find our first parents in a garden. The law was given from Sinai, and its curses were emphasized from the top of Ebal in the open air. The great revival under Ezra began in the open air, as from his pulpit of wood he read the Scriptures and expounded their meaning. The angels gave a snatch of heaven's music and announced the birth of Jesus to the shepherds in the open air. Christ preached His greatest sermon in the open air and proclaimed the gospel to the woman by Jacob's well in the open air. Indeed, most of His miracles and teaching took place in the open air. He did not shun the synagogue nor the upper room, but He delighted in the freedom of the street, the mountain and the plain. His disciples were chosen in the open air. The Apostle Paul was converted in the open air, and no wonder that he became all through his life an open-air preacher, proclaiming from Mars Hill Jesus and the resurrection, and pressing into the market places where the people thronged. Jesus was crucified in the open air, and from the top of Olivet He ascended in the open air. In like manner He shall return with the glory of His Father and the angels in the open air.

EVANGELISM OLD AND NEW

THE FIRST CENTURIES.

All down the ages God has searched for man in the open air. The first mention of church houses is found in the writings of Tertullian at the end of the second century. Justin Martyr was converted by the testimony of an old man preaching in the open air. Raymond Lull, the Spanish nobleman who went as missionary to Africa, preached with the tongue of flame in the open air. Augustine preached to King Ethelbert, of England, in the open air. Wycliffe's poor priests carried on their ministry almost exclusively in the open air. Peter of Bruys would not preach under a roof. Arnold of Brescia stood among the people in the open air and preached until he was thrown into a dungeon from which he went to a martyr's glory. Peter Waldo and the "Poor Men of Lyons" were open-air preachers. The Franciscan, the Dominican and the Cistercian monks preached to the people constantly in the open air. In 1382 there was presented to the Parliament of England by the clergy a complaint against street preaching. John Huss, driven from his pulpit, began the Bohemian reformation in the open air. Luther did most of his work before Diets and with his pen, but it is well known that he preached in the open air at Zwickau to twenty-five thousand people. At Goslar a student from Wittemberg gathered the people under

IN THE OPEN AIR

a lime tree and expounded to them the Scriptures, founding thus a society known as the "Limetree Brethren." John Livingston's great sermon, which resulted in the conversion of five hundred Scotchmen, was delivered during a storm in the open air. Spurgeon says that he preached on the rain and dew, while it was raining, to thousands of people who stood and drank in the words like the thirsty grass. Mr. Kirkham, of England, says that he has frequently preached on the snow in a double sense, standing upon it and talking about it. John Welch held open-air meetings on the Tweed between England and Scotland, and when the Scottish authorities interfered, he would move back again to the English side. As both authorities were not apt to interfere at the same time, he kept up his open-air meetings almost incessantly.

WHITEFIELD AND WESLEY.

The preaching of Whitefield at Kingswood colliery is familiar to every student of the great Methodist revival. Wesley believed that everything should be done decently and in order, and he first thought that preaching in the open air might bring the movement into disrepute; but when he saw the power of the gospel upon these colliery people, he yielded and began himself to preach in the open

EVANGELISM OLD AND NEW

air. When Whitefield left Kingswood for London, his brethren urged him not to carry this innovation with him into the city. He knelt down and asked God to keep him from doing anything rash or unwise; but when he reached London, he could not restrain the fire that burned in his bones, and he was soon standing among the thousands at Moorsfield, preaching to them in a voice of thunder. It is well known that John Wesley was refused his father's pulpit at Epworth. John Taylor stood at the door of the church and announced that Mr. Wesley would preach at six o'clock that evening in the churchyard. Wesley, standing on his father's tomb, preached from the text, "The kingdom of God is not meat and drink, but righteousness and peace and joy in the Holy Ghost." He said afterward: "I am well assured that I did far more good to my Lincolnshire parishioners by preaching three days on my father's tomb than I did by preaching three years in his pulpit." I, for one, rejoice that the Established Church drove Whitefield and Wesley to the fields. The religion of that day needed just such an airing. A short time before his death, Mr. Wesley preached at Winchelsea, when he was eighty-seven years of age, in the open air under an ash tree, afterwards known as "Wesley's Tree."

IN THE OPEN AIR

BETTER THAN POLICEMEN.

The burgomaster of The Hague is reported to have said, "One street preacher is worth ten policemen." Saint Mary's Church in Whitechapel, London, has a pulpit built in the corner on the outside, from which the preacher reaches more people than he can induce to come within. The open air mission, known as Carubber's Close, in Edinburgh, has resulted in the conversion of thousands. Persons on sick beds have heard through open windows the gospel which led them to look up and trust in God. The pastor of the Somerstown Church, in London, declares that two-thirds of his one thousands members were converted in the streets. One of the presbyteries of Great Britain requires that all its ministers shall preach several times during the year in the open air. Bishop Aldhelm, of the seventh century, finding that he could not draw the people to his church, took his harp, and, standing on the corner, played sweetly enough to draw the crowd, and then preached to them the sweeter message of grace. If his spirit should seize the pastors of our city churches and send them out in pleasant weather to their front doorsteps or to an adjoining adjacent lot, they might increase their audiences ten-fold.

EVANGELISM OLD AND NEW

AN EXPERIENCE.

While I was in Liverpool I attended an Episcopal Church one evening, where I heard an earnest sermon on "The Prodigal Son." There were about seventy-five people present; and, as my early education in the Episcopal prayer book had been neglected, I could not keep up with the people as they skipped from page to page. Some persons near me were kind enough to show me the place. The rector took in the situation and looked straight at me most of the time, while he preached earnestly on the dangers of wandering away from God, and the welcome awaiting us at home. Evidently he knew that there were present about seventy-five hardened saints to whom he had preached for years, and, as I did not know the Episcopal prayer book, he took me for a prodigal that needed the gospel, and doubtless the only prodigal who was present. But the surprising part of the service to me was the announcement at the close: "At seven o'clock to-morrow evening the usual open-air service will be held on the steps of this church." Promptly at seven o'clock the next evening I saw the rector open a side gate and come out with several young people carrying a little organ. He placed it on one of the great stone steps and began to play. For three hours that gospel service continued, and not less than twelve

IN THE OPEN AIR

hundred people heard enough truth to take them to heaven if they believed and acted upon it. At the close of the service I asked the rector what results came of this. He replied: "About all the results that come at all come of this. A few children of the church members join, as a matter of course, but those that come in by regeneration are nearly all reached in the open air." The contrast between one poor prodigal on the inside of the church and twelve hundred prodigals on the outside listening to the gospel of Christ made me decide at once that when I reached home I would preach in the open air.

I know that street preaching is not very dignified; but it is well to remember that dignity is not one of the fruits of the Spirit, nor is it classed among the Christian graces. Solomon says: "Folly is set in great dignity." Any fool can be dignified. Dignity has been well defined as the starch of a shroud. If you will look to your right as you enter the Metropolitan Museum in Central Park, New York, you will see one of the most dignified objects in the world. It is the mummy of an Egyptian Prince four thousand year dead. Should you insert a grain of life into it, you would destroy all its dignity in a moment. But life is more important than dignity. We need not the dignified dress parade with high hat, beating drum, and stately march, so much as the smoke and din and glorious confusion of the battle which results in victory for truth and God. And the open air in the streets and fields is the place for such a conflict.

CHAPTER XIV.

THE PRAYER CIRCLE.

Peter and John formed a fraternity of prayer. They were old friends. They had been boys together, and then fishermen on the lake together. They had become Christians about the same time. Peter in the shadow of the denial of his Lord had not gone with John to the crucifixion, but they were together at the open sepulchre. Peter doubtless found in the gentle, loving John a support, and John found in the brave, impulsive Peter an inspiration. They remembered the words of Jesus: "If two of you agree on earth as touching anything that they shall ask, it shall be done for them." After the great revival heavy responsibilities are upon them. They must train the converts and lead the campaign for the evangelization of the world. Answered prayer creates need for more prayer.

POWER OF PRAYER.

While Moses prays Israel prevails, and all great spiritual victories are gained in answer to prayer. Daniel was more powerful than the king because he prayed, and his three friends walked through the fiery furnace in a panoply of prayer. Elijah carried with him the keys that locked the heavens and prevented rain, and with the same key he unlocked the heavens and rain poured upon the earth. When he needed fire out of the heavens he used the same key, and the fire fell upon the altar. While Paul and Silas prayed, the earth shook and the jail doors opened. John Livingston preached and five hundred are converted. He had spent the previous night in prayer. Jonathan Edwards preached and awkwardly held up his manuscript to the light while the people held to the backs of the pews and trembled with fear. A little band of members had been praying all night before, and continued their prayer till the hour of service. Spurgeon's prayers in the little room above his pulpit explained his tongue of fire as he preached to thousands in the Tabernacle. George Muller prayed and six millions of dollars came for the support and training of orphans. Luther was sometimes so busy that he was compelled to spend two or three hours in prayer. His motto was, "To have prayed well is to have studied well." And when Melancthon, his co-worker, died, his knees were calloused from much kneeling.

God works in answer to prayer. Let Peter and John keep together. Form circles of prayer as the means of obtaining what you need.

THE PRAYER CIRCLE

PRAYER AND WORK.

Learn from the experience of Peter and John three things:

1. God uses men who unite work with prayer. While the eyes of Peter and John are up toward God, their hands are toward their suffering fellows. They do not make prayer a substitute for work, nor work a substitute for prayer. The man at the beautiful gate had to be carried by his friends. That was the best they could do for him, and such help was not to be despised. It put him in the way of supporting himself in his poverty. There are people who have to be carried, and it blesses those who carry them. There are wives whose afflicted husbands have to be carried. But love does not complain. To earn a support it goes to the store with a song and returns at night with a smile. Carrying others may make us strong. Their weakness develops our strength. There are others, however, who have to be carried because of their sins. The burden of a drunken husband has crushed the hope and then the life out of many a faithful wife. Not a few shiftless, wayward children must be carried through life by long-suffering parents. But the faith of Peter and John did more for the man in a moment than his kind friends had done for him in years.

EVANGELISM OLD AND NEW

GAIN OR LOSS?

Peter lifted the lame man up and he stood as if he were trying his new ankles; then he walked, and when he found he could stand and walk, he began to leap and praise God. He was too happy to behave. The staid conventionalism of the temple worship could not express his feelings. His antics attracted a crowd and got the apostles into trouble, but he could not help it. Time was when men and women would shout "Hallelujah!" and clap their hands for joy. They felt that God had done so much for them that they could but praise Him. We have lost this confusion in the temple. The nap of the deacon in the corner is never disturbed by a shout. Is the loss a gain? Does your joy express itself in more quiet ways, or is there no joy to express? Has rigid conventionalism frozen out grace? May God melt the ice and make the water of exultant joy flow out, even if it makes a little noise in flowing.

A pope remarked to Aquinas as they stood by a table covered with gold. "The church need say no longer, 'Silver and gold have I none.'" "Yes," remarked the cardinal, "but the church has not the power to say, 'Rise up and walk.'" In gaining gold there has been a loss of power. It is better to be poor in gold and rich in grace than poor in

THE PRAYER CIRCLE

grace and rich in gold. The gold may be used for God's glory, but the grace is His glory.

TAKING THE DEVIL BY SURPRISE.

Peter and John took the Devil by surprise. The healing of the man was not on the program. Our programs for revivals the Devil knows how to interrupt. He is certain to start rival attractions. It is well to take him by surprise. Let the program go, while you do what comes in the way. The prayer in the temple can wait while you stop on the way and win a soul for Christ. This newly-won soul may go into the temple with you and give life to the meeting. Be ready for emergencies by living all the time in fellowship with God.

SPIRITUAL NEEDS.

2. God works through men who magnify the needs of the soul. The healing of the man's ankle bones was an incidental matter. It was used simply as a church bell for calling the people together. Peter and John do not set themselves up as faith healers and invite people to bring their sick. In a sermon that follows nothing is said about the physical needs of the multitude. They are urged to repent of their sins and save their souls. The salvation of the soul is the final salvation of the body.

And Jesus, the great Healer, did not magnify physical healing. He told some who were healed to say nothing about it. He knew that such physical healing could be counterfeited. The magicians can do so with their enchantments. Christian Science—which is opposed in its vagaries to both Christianity and science—bases its claims for acceptance on its power to heal disease. And almost every modern heresy makes the same claim.

The apostles healed many sick people, but in their preaching the salvation of the soul was their single thought and purpose.

FULL SALVATION.

3. God works through men who, while they pray, preach a full Saviour. The cross with its blood is in the front. Peter never leaves out the crucifixion. "Without the shedding of blood there is no remission." A Saviour without nail prints is an imposter. Sinners need, first of all, forgiveness, and it can be had only through Christ on the cross.

Peter also magnifies the resurrection of Christ. The two things go together. When a man makes little of the death of Christ, he is certain to make little of the resurrection. If His death was an episode, His resurrection was a myth, a restoration of suspended animation, or some other device of unbelief. He rejects the alphabet, and cannot,

THE PRAYER CIRCLE

of course, read. He rejects the life that comes through death, and cannot grow. He cannot unlock the treasures of truth because he has thrown away the key. The unbelief that makes our Lord only a hero in meeting death, because He could not help it, makes Him very commonplace everywhere else.

Having proclaimed the death and resurrection of Jesus, Peter now fills them with hope by pointing believers to "the times of the restoration of all things," which will take place when Jesus returns in glory. Restoring the impotent man's ankle bones is a prophecy of the time when all ankle bones shall be restored. Jesus restored eyes, muscles, nerves, morals and minds. His miracles of healing were simply an earnest of the complete restoration of the whole being when the Lord of life shall appear. This blessed hope inspires us, while we pray, work and wait for the salvation of the lost.

CHAPTER XV.

THE WIDENING VISION.

If you have ever climbed a high mountain, you remember that you started in the shadows of the trees at the base, where there was little or no outlook. You could see a few hundred yards around you, but after a while you rose above the tops of the trees and looked out upon a beautiful landscape. As you climbed higher, the fields and the running streams appeared, but you could see only one-half of the horizon; the other half was shut off by the mountain. But when you reached the top, you found yourself in a great circular room, bounded by the horizon on all sides, carpeted with green, and bordered with curtains of crimson and gold.

THE BROADER HORIZON.

Such is the experience of the Christian. When he is first converted, he looks about him for someone he may lead to Christ. You feel specially drawn in sympathy and prayer toward those whom you love best; but after you have grown in grace, you rise above the treetops of mere selfish love, you take in a wider view, you begin to pray and work for the salvation of the community, and, as

THE WIDENING VISION

you rise still higher in spiritual life, the outlook widens, you pray for your state, your country, the people of your own tongue.

But you have not reached the mountain top of vision until you have taken the view of Christ, which sweeps the whole horizon of earth. You pray and work and give now for the salvation, not of your own family or community or state, but of the world. Such is the widening vision of Acts 1:8: "Witnesses first in Jerusalem," your home, your business, among your intimate friends, then "in all Judea," the town or state about you; then "in Samaria," the surrounding country; and then "to the uttermost part of the earth."

PETER AND PAUL.

It is interesting to see how God widened the vision of the Apostles and the early Christians. Pentecost was a Jewish revival; there was not one Gentile convert, so far as we know. Peter was the apostle to the Jews, and seemed to care not for the salvation of anyone else until in the vision at Joppa he saw the sheet let down from heaven, filled with animals clean and unclean, and the call came, "Rise, Peter, slay and eat." He remonstrated, because he was not in the habit, being a Jew, of eating such animals. "What God hath cleansed call not thou common," was the answer

EVANGELISM OLD AND NEW

to his remonstrance. And that housetop in Joppa becomes unto Peter the mountain-top of vision. He sees beyond Jerusalem and Judea into Samaria and "the uttermost part of the earth."

God took the Apostle Paul at once to the mountain-top, and gave him the larger vision of the Gospel's message. The world was his parish. While he slept amid the historic associations of Troy, he was not thinking of the great siege, or the wooden horse, or the flight of Aeneas. His purpose was thrusting him forward into the regions beyond. He heard the call of the man in Macedonia, "Come over and help us," and he was not "disobedient unto the heavenly vision." The old farmer who prayed, "God bless me and my wife, my son John and his wife, us four and no more," had made up his mind to live and die among the shades of the trees at the base of the mountain. He never rose above their tops. He saw no vision beyond his barn and fields.

King James, learning of the poverty of Ben Jonson, sent him five shillings. Jonson said to the messenger, "The King sends me five shillings because I live in an alley. Tell him that his soul lives in an alley" We do not admire the ingratitude of Jonson, but we are impressed by the fact that the soul of a king can live in an alley, and the man who does not believe in foreign missions, con-

THE WIDENING VISION

tending that the gospel should be preached only to those just about him, has a soul living in an alley. He should move out into the broad avenues of larger purpose and greater sacrifice for Christ.

SHATTERED AND SCATTERED.

The early church was slow to learn this lesson. The apostles decided to remain at Jerusalem. They doubtless argued that the capitol city ought to be christianized first of all; that there was enough work to do at home; thousands of Jews under the shadow of the Temple were not Christians, and there was no need of going further until the work was completed here. But in the language of Dr. Pierson, "God shattered the church that He might scatter it." Persecutions began. The head of James fell from the block. The cozy nest was stirred in order that the eaglets of the gospel might be made to fly into the regions beyond. The private members of the church went everywhere preaching the gospel.

But after a century or two the church settled back into its lethargy. She became rich and contented. Married to the state, there was for her no lack of funds and influence. Aggressive missionary work ceased, and the period that followed is known as the Dark Ages. Night settled upon the world. Some stars pierced the gloom, but

EVANGELISM OLD AND NEW

there was no sunrise for nearly a thousand years. God's church was content to live among the shadows at the base of the mountain. She refused to climb to the top and behold the vision of her Lord. She looked after her self interest, and as a result there arose within her a spirit of bitter controversy, which soon blazed out into fires of cruel persecution.

RAYMOND LULL.

The first man who seemed to awake in this night of lethargy from the sleep of death was Raymund Lull, a Spanish nobleman who lived in the thirteenth century. He caught a vision of Christ for the world. He covenanted with God in the words, "To thee, O Lord God, I offer myself, my wife, my children, and all that I possess." He established missionary training schools, where Arabic and other languages were taught to the young men. His ambition was nothing less than the subjection of the Moslem world to Jesus. Cast into prison and then driven out of his country, he was undaunted. Like Christopher Columbus, he went from court to court, urging pope and king and prince to enter upon the crusade. "No church," says Dr. George Smith, "papal or reformed, has produced a missionary so original in plan, so arduous and persevering in execution, so varied in gifts, so inspired by the love of Christ, as this saint

THE WIDENING VISION

of seventy-nine whom Mohammedans stoned to death on the thirteenth of June, 1315, In an age of violence and faithlessness, he was the apostle of heavenly love." His last words as he knelt on the sands of Africa, while his murderers were stoning him, were "Jesus only."

FRANCIS XAVIER.

The next man who rose above the tree-tops and caught a vision of world-wide missions was Francis Xavier, who lived in the sixteenth century. His early associations were with Protestants, from whom he learned salvation by grace, and through their teaching he doubtless passed from death unto life. But in after years he came under the hypnotic influence of Ignatius Loyola, with whom he formed the Order of the Jesuits, and vowed to obey man rather than God. In his methods he was an ecclesiastic, making Christians by sprinkling water on their heads. In one month he converted in this way ten thousand natives of Travancore, and after ten years' work he claimed converts by the million. It is true that the religion of such converts evaporated as rapidly as the water on their heads, and his mania for counting led Xavier to ridiculous extremes. But however we may condemn his fanaticism, his folly, and his heresy, we can but admire his missionary zeal.

EVANGELISM OLD AND NEW

Looking toward China, he exclaimed in the delirium of fever, "O rock, rock, when wilt thou open to my Master?" His dreams were of the world subdued to Christ, and he would spring up in the night, shouting. "Yet more, O my God, yet more!" His motto, "Ad majorem dei gloriam" (To the greater glory of God) would be a good watchword for all Christendom.

A DEFECT IN THE REFORMATION.

The reformation of the sixteenth century under Luther, Zwingli, and Calvin, was a revival of doctrines which gave to the church a wider and clearer vision of truth, but in the matter of foreign missions left the people of God still among the shadows of the trees at the base of the mountain. The efforts of the Reformers strengthened the things that remained, without reaching out to the heathen world, and the danger is when we simply try to strengthen the things that remain we will after a while have on hand only "remains." The church of Christ can have a vigorous life only as she takes in His vision of grace for all men.

JOHN ELIOT.

During the seventeenth century there are indications of missionary awakening. John Eliot, driven by persecution from his native land, comes

THE WIDENING VISION.

to America and spends his life preaching to the Indians. Through thirty-eight years he toiled and gathered not less than thirty-six hundred converts into fourteen settlements, with twenty-four native preachers, who carried on the work.

BARTHOLOMEW ZIEGENBALG.

The eighteenth century finds a large portion of the church of Christ far above the tree-tops, with a broad vision of obligation and privilege spread out before them. A mother in Denmark, while dying, bequeathed to her children at her bedside a great treasure which she urged them to seek in the Bible. "You will find it there," she said, "and there is not a page I have not wet with my tears." One of these children was Bartholomew Ziegenbalg, who became the pioneer Protestant missionary to India. In spite of almost insurmountable obstacles he mastered the Tamil language, made grammar and lexicon, and translated the Bible into that tongue. When dying, he caught a vision of the glory beyond, and shading his eyes with his hands, he exclaimed, "How is it so bright, as if the sun shone full in my face?" He then requested those about him to sing his favorite hymn, and he went into the presence of God on the wings of song.

EVANGELISM OLD AND NEW.

ZINZENDORF.

The brave spirit of John Huss, the Bohemian martyr, was in his followers, who found in Count Zinzendorf a leader and patron. Zinzendorf, when a child of four years, was heard to pray, "Dear Saviour, be thou mine, and I will be thine." He wrote letters to Jesus, and threw them out of the window, expecting that He would read and answer them. He formed the "Order of the Grain of Mustard Seed," whose object was to sow the seeds of truth in the hearts of others. As he grew in stature and grace, he said, "I have one passion. It is He, and He alone." In marriage covenant he agreed with his devoted bride to renounce rank, to make a consecration of wealth and a complete dedication of self to the Lord. It was on their wedding tour that they found those Moravian exiles and established the settlement at Herrnhutt. This little band, known as the Moravian Church, has been a flame of missionary zeal. With about fifty thousand members in Christendom, they have won to Christ one hundred and seventy-five thousand in heathendom. Their plan was to take the gospel to those who needed it most, and seek to save the most degraded. It was at this fire that Wesley and Whitefield lit their torches of evengelistic zeal.

THE WIDENING VISION

CHRISTIAN SCHWARTZ.

In Germany another Christian mother lay dying, and, turning to her husband, said, "For this child I prayed, and the Lord hath given me my petition which I asked for him. So long as he liveth he shall be lent to the Lord. Take him and foster him in any aptitude which he may show for the Christian ministry. This is my last legacy." We are not surprised that Christian Schwartz, with such a mother breathing during her last hours such a prayer, should follow Ziegenbalg into India as a herald of the cross. He lived Christ among the natives, and won the confidence of all. When Hyder Ali was told that the English would send an ambassador to treat with him, he replied, "Send to me none of your agents, for I trust neither their words nor pledges, but send me the Christian missionary and I will receive him."

WILLIAM CAREY.

The church in England had not risen above the tree-tops. It was living in the shadows of its own self seeking. The preachers were much occupied with splitting theological hairs, and there was little progress. One man had climbed to the top and had caught the vision of Christ as the Saviour of the World. As he sat on his cobbler's bench, he looked upon the map spread before him, with the heathen countries blackened by charcoal. When he spoke to a company of ministers about preaching the gospel to the heathen, a learned man arose and said, "Young man, sit down. When God wants to convert the heathen He will do it without your help or mine." But even this learned minister could not drag William Carey from his mountain-top of vision down to the shadows of selfishness again. Being invited to preach at an association, he took for his subject, "Expect great things from God; attempt great things for God." A few like Andrew Fuller came up to the mountain-top with him and were stirred to the depths of their souls by the widening vision.

JUDSON AND RICE.

In America the church was asleep in the shadows. One young man, Samuel J. Mills, had risen above the tree-tops, and he gathered about him other young men, who met and prayed that God would open the way for them to take the gospel to the heathen world. Out of this prayer-meeting was born the foreign Missionary organization among the Congregationalists, who sent Adoniram Judson and Luther Rice as their missionaries to India. On the way Judson, while reading his Greek New Testament, became convinced that he ought to be immersed. Luther Rice, travelling on

THE WIDENING VISION

another ship, came to the same decision, and on their arrival in India they sought Baptist preachers and were "buried with Christ in baptism." This, of course, cut them off from their Congregationalist brethren at home, but it threw them upon the Baptist churches of America, who had no foreign missionary organization. Out of this grew the modern foreign missionary movement among the Baptists of America, which has done a mighty work in lifting the churches at home from the shadows at the base of the mountain to the summit of vision.

As we read the record of this world-wide missionary work by all denominations, we have a widening vision of the gospel's power, and every lover of his race who knows the record of these facts can but exclaim, "Glory to God in the highest, and on earth peace and good will among men," while he stands on the mountain-top of vision, praying, giving and working for the evangelization of the world.

www.ingramcontent.com/pod-product-compliance
Lightning Source LLC
Chambersburg PA
CBHW070316230426
43663CB00011B/2154